True
Spooky Stories
of Hawai'i

EDITED BY
RICK CARROLL

THE BESS PRESS
P.O. Box 22388
Honolulu, Hawai'i 96823

Cataloging-in-Publication Data

Carroll, Rick
    Chicken skin : true spooky stories of Hawaiʻi / edited by Rick Carroll.
        p.   cm.
    Includes illustrations.
    ISBN 1-57306-055-0
    1. Ghost stories, American - Hawaii.
2. Tales - Hawaii.   3. Legends - Hawaii.
I. Title.
GR580.H3.C37 1996   398.25-dc20

Passages from the *Kumulipo* in the Introduction are from Beckwith, Martha
Warren, trans. and ed. *The Kumulipo: A Hawaiian Creation Chant.*
Honolulu: University of Hawaiʻi Press, 1972.

Every effort has been made to trace the ownership of all material in this book
and to obtain permission for its use.

Printed in the United States of America

First printing, September 1996

ISBN 1-57306-055-0

Table of Contents

Do you have a chicken skin story you'd like to share?
Selected stories will appear in a future book.
Write to Chicken Skin,
c/o The Bess Press, P. O. Box 22388,
Honolulu, HI 96823
or e-mail rcarroll@pixi.com

To Kuʻulei Nitahara and all the souls of the dearly departed . . .

No anthology leaps to print. It begins as a vision, then slowly grows in direct response to individual enthusiasm, creativity, and generosity. Otherwise, we are only staring out to sea, waiting. To those who made this book a reality—Buddy Bess and editor Revé Shapard at The Bess Press; Nanette Purnell of The Cemetery Research Project; Jean Kent Campbell, whose *Nā Moʻolelo ʻŌkala: Eerie Stories of Hawaiʻi* added genuine lustre; and every contributor, especially Akoni Akana, Don Chapman, Lei-Ann Stender Durant, Leslie Ann Hayashi, James D. Houston, Victoria Nelson, Lee Quarnstrom, and Emme Tomimbang— all I can say now is *mahalo nui loa*, and be careful out there.

About the Author

Rick Carroll is the author of six books on Hawai'i, including the award-winning *Great Outdoor Adventures of Hawaii* and the new Frommer's *Hawaii 1997 Guide*. A former daily journalist with the *San Francisco Chronicle*, he covered Hawai'i and the Pacific as a special correspondent for United Press International. He now writes about Hawai'i for Macmillan Travel, New York, and serves as contributing editor of *ALOHA: The Magazine of Hawai'i and the Pacific.*® He lives at Lanikai Beach on O'ahu's windward side.

Introduction

Fear falls upon me on the mountain top
Fear of the passing night
Fear of the night approaching
Fear of the pregnant night
Fear of the breach of the law
Dread of the place of offering and the narrow trail
Dread of the food and the waste part remaining
Dread of the receding night
Awe of the night approaching . . .

— from the *Kumulipo*, Hawaiian creation chant

If you live in Hawai'i or visit often, you've probably experienced chicken skin, that hair-raising, skin-tingling sensation known elsewhere as goose bumps. What made you tingle may have been something otherworldly, something you can never explain. Until now these strange encounters were written on the wind, remnants of Hawai'i's oral tradition. Or they were whispered in confidence to friends. Such stories were rarely written down and were published in only a handful of scholarly publications.

In *Chicken Skin: True Spooky Stories of Hawai'i* you will read for the first time authentic stories about haunted houses and *heiau*, *'aumākua* and ancient bones, night marchers and Nu'uanu noises, ghosts in graveyards and on golf courses. Some stories are as current as today's headlines. See "H-3 Collapse a Mystery." All give rise to that spine-tingling sensation known in Hawai'i as chicken skin.

The stories in this anthology are by two dozen authors: native Hawaiians, including *kupuna* Danny Akaka and *kumu hula* Akoni Akana; nationally known writers Steve Heller, James D. Houston, and Victoria Nelson; scientists and skeptics, frequent visitors and local residents, who have all experienced chicken skin in Hawai'i.

FIRST ENCOUNTERS

My own chicken skin encounters in Hawai'i began one summer on Maui twenty years ago when I first met my calabash cousins in upcountry Kula. My sister, Conni, married Ben Keau, Jr., the eldest son of the Keau family, on a warm day on the San Francisco peninsula, and the reception was almost as good as going to Maui. Although I had been to Hawai'i many times before, I had never been to Maui, and Ben kept urging me to see his island. In the summer of 1976, I arrived on Maui to meet the members of the Keau family, both living and dead. I didn't exactly meet the dead, but Ben Keau, Sr., the patriarch of the family, did take me to family graves in Kula, Hāna and Ke'anae, where he was born 100 percent Hawaiian in the early 1900s. He took me, sometimes after dark, to family graves to introduce me to past generations. In old Maui graveyards I realized with a shiver that spirits are very much alive in Hawai'i in ways few on the mainland can comprehend.

Some years later, I took leave of the *San Francisco Chronicle* and bought a one-way ticket to Hawai'i to pursue the fabled writer's life in the Pacific, complete with an early laptop computer under a royal palm at Lanikai Beach. New friends and total strangers, by way of introducing me to the islands and as a kind of gentle initiation, I suppose, soon told me unbelievable stories about supernatural, mysterious, inexplicable things.

Like night marchers in Olomana who passed though a

house one night and caused one of the occupants to be temporarily paralyzed. And *Fantasia*-inspired centipedes that exploded into a hundred tiny centipedes when slashed by a machete. Or how Hawai'i's sharks may be somebody's uncle. Some stories sounded so much like campfire tales of my youth that I dismissed them with a laugh. Others, obviously folkloric, reminded me of stories by people who live close to nature. Still others were so haunting I never forgot them. Of people "praying" you to death, of secret caves full of old canoes and feathered capes of long-dead *ali'i*. Of fishhooks made of the bones of defeated warriors. And night marchers who walked ancient paths to conduct rituals and ceremonies.

On assignments in the South Pacific I encountered spirits strong enough to lean on—in the shadow of Tahai, the giant stone statue at Hanga Roa on Easter Island, at Opunohou, the sacrificial marae overlooking Cook's Bay on Moorea, and on the island of Huahine, where our guides, afraid of lingering evil spirits, refused to ascend sacred Mount Matairea beyond a gigantic banyan tree hung with skulls two centuries ago—all of which I initially dismissed as native superstition, the island version of urban myths.

All the stories had one thing in common: they produced a frisson of excitement, that little tingle up and down your spine, or the raised hair on the nape of your neck, that delicious shiver people in Hawai'i call chicken skin. Perfect example: A local friend celebrated her 30th birthday recently in the garden of the courtyard at Honolulu's Bernice Pauahi Bishop Museum and later discovered strangers in the background of every photograph taken that night. The uninvited guests looked like stern-faced New England haoles from another era.

Not all chicken skin stories are scary; some are delightfully funny, others poignant, like Auntie Irmgard Aluli, at Mauna Kea Beach Hotel's (re)opening-night luau on Kauna'oa Bay on the Big Island, singing "One More Round."

Others are simply amazing. At a party in a *kama'āina* home one night I picked up from an end table an ornate fountain pen inlaid with silver and mother of pearl and started to doodle and felt an eerie sensation—only to learn in the next moment that the pen was Queen Lili'uokalani's own, perhaps the very one she used to write her songs.

Hawai'i's abundant sensational nature often gives rise to chicken skin. I have experienced chicken skin while walking on red-hot flowing lava as it ran into the sea near Kamoamoa one night, observing a night rainbow on Maui on Mā'alaea Bay, while tracing my fingers in the stone petroglyphs at Puakō on the Big Island's Kohala Coast, wandering, alone, in the half-light of Wao Kele O Puna rain forest, hearing chants at sundown one night at Pohukaina Mound on the grounds of 'Iolani Palace. It all could just be my writerly imagination, but I don't think so.

You don't even have to be in Hawai'i to experience chicken skin. In a San Francisco apartment with a panoramic view of the bay, I stood gazing on Alcatraz, thinking of Hawai'i, wishing I were there, when the radio began to play "E Ala Ē," that haunting sovereignty anthem by Israel Kamakawiwo'ole, and the song and his voice and the moment made me shiver.

When total strangers stand holding hands at public gatherings, singing "Aloha 'Oe," I get a little chicken skin. It probably happens to you, too.

COLLECTING CHICKEN SKIN

I started collecting chicken skin stories, writing down favorites, logging them in my laptop intending some day to do something with them, a magazine article, maybe, or a collection of stories, a goal unrealized until now.

My stories took a serendipitous spin in an Oʻahu graveyard a dozen years ago, although I didn't know it at the time. In 1984, I met Nanette Purnell, then setting out to make a census of the dead in Hawaiʻi's graveyards by recording the names she found carved on tombstones. I wrote a story about Nanette and The Cemetery Research Project that appeared in the *Honolulu Advertiser* and was picked up by the national media; it even made "The CBS Evening News with Dan Rather." Last year when *Midweek* editor Don Chapman (his "Ghostly Golf" will give you pause) asked me to contribute a chicken skin story for Halloween, I eschewed the usual recitation of ghost yarns to write a cover profile on Nanette and her accomplishments, and I included a few of my favorite chicken skin stories, among them "Old Hawaiian Graveyards," which appears in this anthology.

The article apparently touched a bundle of nerves and brought phone calls, including one from Revé Shapard, an engaging editor at Bess Press, then at work on a book of Chicken Skin stories. She already had a remarkable oral history project by Jean Kent Campbell, who had interviewed scores of Hawaiian storytellers for *Nā Moʻolelo ʻŌkala: Eerie Stories of Hawaiʻi,* her senior honor thesis at the University of Hawaiʻi-Mānoa. Now, Revé wanted my collection, and someone to put them all together. I couldn't say no. After we decided to include the best selections of *Nā Moʻolelo ʻŌkala* with a few of my favorite stories, along with excerpts from historic references, I set out in search of new, original contemporary stories by local and national authors and then we folded them all into a book, which you now hold in your hands.

Each story had to pass several tests: it had to be true, it had to be derived from Hawai'i and, this is most important, it had to produce chicken skin.

Another key element surfaced along the way. The authors, for the most part, turned out to be skeptics who nevertheless had encountered situations in Hawai'i they still can't explain. That, alone, is what makes this collection unique and fascinating to me. These aren't old ghost stories or campfire tales or even myths and legends; these are true stories of extraordinary phenomena experienced by ordinary disbelievers.

Many people, when I told them what I was doing, were at first reluctant to come forward and tell their stories in public. Others readily volunteered intriguing leads. Cheryl Tsutsumi's brother had seen the high-rise ghost in downtown Honolulu's Pacific Tower. From George Kanahele I learned of ghosts that steal your voice. Jocelyn Fujii's sister saw a woman walk above the beach at Hanalei. Sheila Donnelly knew of a room in a Waikīkī hotel that's haunted by the ghost of a Japanese woman who jumped to her death from the lanai. After she swore me to secrecy, Emme Tomimbang told me chicken skin stories you wouldn't believe. It was quite amazing. Soon I had ghost stories coming out my ears. I had collected more stories than I could tell in a single evening.

MANY VOICES, MANY VIEWPOINTS

What we have here is more than just another book about ghosts; in fact, ghosts play only a cameo role in *Chicken Skin*, which also features animism, primal fears, old and new taboos (or *kapu*, as we say in the Islands) and elements of nature, the sky, sea and earth, with a little myth and legend to keep it all in context. *Chicken Skin: True Spooky Stories of Hawai'i* is the story of old and new Hawai'i, told by many people in many voices from many points of view.

Local residents Danny Akaka, Akoni Akana, Louise Aloy, Pat Bacon, Ed Chang, Lei-Ann Stender Durant, Leslie Ann Hayashi, and Pam Soderberg, and former resident Mark Allen Howard contributed original chicken skin stories of contemporary Hawai'i. The late Mary Kawena Pukui is represented with "The Marchers of the Night," which tells you how to survive an encounter. Nicholas Love ("My Grandfather's Ghosts"), who is the son of *kumu hula* Maunalei Love, is the youngest contributor, only twelve, but already an accomplished Hawaiian storyteller.

Scientists Phil Helfrich and Bernard G. Mendonca and naturalist Rob Pacheco contributed amazing true accounts even they are hard-pressed to explain.

And otherwise doubting journalists from Hawai'i and California like Burl Burlingame, Don Chapman, Gordon Morse, Lee Quarnstrom, and Emme Tomimbang contributed investigative reports and personal experiences.

Chicken Skin is a different sort of book; it goes beyond folklore into an untapped realm that you will discover when you read these personal accounts, preferably alone. An interactive anthology, this book I know will give you chicken skin. Here's a preview to show you what I mean:

- Scientists go in search of a deadly seaweed in a Hāna tidepool and discover a lethal substance ancient Hawaiians already knew and used in daily life.

- Hawaiian *pueo* (owls) gather at high noon on Moloka'i as a woman lies dying. A white dog shows itself many times high atop Mauna Loa. A gray cat leads school children to the altar of forbidden Pi'ilani *heiau*.

• A woman talks to a rock that blocks a construction project in Wai'anae. Bulldozers mysteriously overturn at a golf course construction site.

• Someone watches over the sacrificial altar of Pu'uomahuka *heiau* on O'ahu's North Shore. A baby has nightly conversations with an ancient Hawaiian tribe.

CHICKEN SKIN IN LITERATURE

Chicken skin stories in Hawai'i have always been popular. For more than a century numerous authors have contributed to the genre. While browsing in the library of the Bishop Museum I came upon an 1893 collection of ghost stories entitled *Seeing Thousands of Ghosts for a Single Night at Leilono*. (Leilono was a leaping-off place for spirits in what today is Moanalua Valley.) The manuscript, translated by Mary Kawena Pukui, is one of the earliest known collections of ghost stories written in Hawai'i, some of the stories dating from 1863. I was cheered to note that it begins like this: "Because of the many requests of the readers who have enjoyed these stories, therefore the rest are being issued . . . ."

One story, "The Battered Ships of Alenuihaha," describes how frightened passengers on an interisland ferry spotted the ghost canoes of Kamehameha I on his way to wage war against Kahekili in the famous battle of 'Iao and Kepaniwai. "Goose pimples rose on every one on board and some actually cried," the author noted.

In 1915, William Drake Westervelt, a historian of renown and diligent student of Hawaiian folklore, collected eighteen legends in a neat little book now out of print entitled *Hawaiian Legends of Ghosts and Ghost-Gods*.

In 1955, Katharine Luomala, an anthropologist, presented the scholarly work *Voices on the Wind, Polynesian Myths and Chants*, which the late Dr. A. Grove Day, professor emeritus of English, University of Hawai'i, called "the best modern literary treatment of Polynesian poetry."

In 1977, *Hawai'i Tales of Yesterday: A Collection of Legends and Stories*, by Roland Lalana Kapahukaniolono, featured twenty-three stories about sharks, *paniolo*, and mermaids.

In 1986, Day and Dr. Bacil F. Kirtley, author of *A Motif-Index of Traditional Polynesian Narratives*, gathered up thirty-four historical and literary essays by Robert Dean Frisbee, James Norman Hall, Jack London, W. Somerset Maugham, Robert Louis Stevenson, and Mark Twain and called it *Horror in Paradise: Grim and Uncanny Tales from Hawaii and the South Seas.*

In 1994, historian and teacher Glen Grant published supernatural tales of Japanese ghosts in his book *Obake: Ghost Stories in Hawai'i.*

While the body of ghostly literature in Hawai'i is dominated by academics, the mainstream of true personal experience has until now gone untapped.

SEEN ONE, LATELY?

No place I have ever lived is so haunted by spirits, real or imagined, and in such a diverse array. There are as many different ghosts here as there are ethnic groups. Hawai'i's ghosts are known by many names. Hawaiians call them *wailua*. They also have many names for chicken skin: *'ōkala, 'ōkakala, lī ka 'ili, lī ka 'i'o, kūhulukū, kakalaiō*. To the Japanese, ghosts are *obake*; to Filipinos, *awangs*; to Koreans, *kwi shin*; and to Chinese, *qui*. All can cause serious chicken skin.

Hawai'i's ghosts are very cosmopolitan. Hawaiians have Madame Pele, whose face is regularly seen in the fire pits of Halema'uma'u. Chinese have phantoms that steal out of the underworld. Japanese worship the spirits of their ancestors during Obon. Filipinos see rose petals fall from the sky. Everybody in the islands carves toothy grins on pumpkins each October in a vestigial reenactment of Druid rites.

Hawaiian night walkers march in remote valleys, sometimes through suburban Honolulu neighborhoods; a ghost stalks the Pali Highway, the ghost of the wife of Sen. Leland Stanford, founder of Stanford University, haunts the Moana Hotel. There's even a sea-going ghost aboard the interisland cruise ship S.S. *Independence.*

Ghosts of Hawaiians past regularly put a halt to construction projects. On Maui, The Ritz-Carlton Kapalua had to move its proposed multimillion dollar beachfront hotel back from the beach when bulldozers uncovered a mass grave in coastal sand dunes. The popular hotel avoided the wrath of displaced spirits by dedicating the graveyard as a memorial.

Hilo Airport, I have been told countless times, is haunted, which is why most flights arrive and depart from Keahole Airport on the Big Island's Kailua-Kona side.

There are ghosts at Leinaaka'uhane, or Ghost's Leap, on O'ahu's Wai'anae Coast, where souls of ancient Hawaiians departed for the netherworld; and there's definitely a peace-loving ghost in Mānoa Chinese Cemetery who keeps breaking those noisy leaf blowers.

There are so many ghosts wandering about in Hawai'i it's a wonder there's room for the living. When people die in Hawai'i, their spirits must be reluctant to leave this earthly paradise. Which reminds me of that old joke about the Hawaiian couple who reach the gates of Heaven. "Where did you live?"

"Hawai'i."

"Oh, dear," the angel says, "You're going to be disappointed."

The cultural diversity of Hawai'i is matched only by that of its spirit world. In the early 1970s, Victoria Nelson (her contribution to *Chicken Skin* is "An Informal Census of Moloka'i Ghosts") asked her University of Hawai'i students to write down a few ghost stories. "This assignment presented absolutely no problem for anyone," she recalls in *My Time in Hawai'i: A Polynesian Memoir*, one of my favorite accounts of contemporary life in the Islands. "O'ahu, I now discovered, had its own legacy of the supernatural, and we soon assembled an impressive collection of the old standbys familiar to any O'ahu teenager: the dead man hanging from the tree at Morgan's Corner, the Chinese woman with no face at the Waialae Drive-In, assorted spooks at Mānoa Cemetery, the latter seemingly a "terror place" of the first order. . . .

"The most frequent explanation given for apparitions was not 'coming back' to family and friends but the more depersonalized, abstract theme of violated graveyard: 'This structure (Hilo Airport, or whatever) was built on an old burial ground.'"

"Each group has its own ghost stories," says historian Barbara Wong, who researches, writes and tells ancient Chinese ghost stories, and also researches multicultural ghost stories—including Hawaiian, Japanese and Filipino. "Some may be more frightening to one culture than another. Some things in Filipino stories are terrifying—there's a type of ghost that lives off human flesh; it appears during the day, spears the body and flies away."

"No matter what culture," she says, "what's frightening in one group is frightening in another. Everybody loves a ghost story.

"We are delighted with fear. It's a way to experience fear but know you're safe. Even for adults that's true. You get adrenaline pumping but you know you're going to come out okay. The unknown is fascinating. We are all mystified and intrigued by things nobody can explain."

None of the stories you are about to read can be fully explained. They defy logic and reason and scientific explanation. Are they supernatural? Perhaps. Paranormal? Who really knows? All I know for certain is they will give you chicken skin. Guaranteed.

Fear falls upon me on the mountain top
Fear of the passing night . . .
Dread of the receding night
Awe of the night approaching . . .

Heiau

Ghosts of Hula Past

Things Go Bump in the Night

Watched

Cliffside Burial Caves of Waipi'o Valley

On Kaua'i's north shore on a knoll above the boulders of Kē'ē Beach stands a sacred altar of rocks, often draped with flower leis and ti leaf offerings. This altar, dedicated to Laka, the goddess of hula, may seem like a primal relic from the days of idols, but Ka Ulu o Laka Heiau is very much in use today. Often, dancers, men and women, of Hawai'i's hula *hālau* (schools) climb the cliff, bearing small gifts of flowers. Sometimes, a mother of a newborn will deposit the umbilical cord of her infant at this sacred shrine in a revival of the old Hawaiian ways, once banned by missionaries. In Hawaiian myths, Lohi'au, a handsome chief, danced here before the fire goddess Pele, and their passion became Hā'ena, which means "the heat." The site is filled with what Hawaiians call *mana,* or power. If you climb the cliff to visit this altar you will discover that you don't have to be Hawaiian to experience *mana*. But you must be *very* careful what you say and do.

Ghosts of Hula Past

This was at Kēʻē down near Hāʻena, the hula platform over there. I was invited. My cousin is a *kumu hula* on Kauaʻi and they had their *hōʻike* for his *hālau* and there was a fund-raiser, a *hōʻike*, so he said come up. This was about eight, ten years ago. I had *keiki hālau* over here on Maui so he told me come up and do something, so we practiced over here real hard for that show, 'cause I was really excited about doing it. They was having it at Kauaʻi Civic Center.

And when we went to Kauaʻi I told the kids already that we was going to go visit the *hula pā* at Kēʻē before we go, you know, sometime before we do this show for them. So one morning we woke up early, no, we had a practice first. We had practice and, ho, they was just all off, and everybody was making me mad, was real, you know, I was yelling at them already, you guys, you did so well back on Maui, you come over here practicing, you so *moloā* all this kind. So we was feeling all junk but then I said, o.k., we go out Kēʻē. So we all jumped in the van and went out there.

Had four mothers, five *keiki*, myself, and we went to Kēʻē and we hiked up to the top and then I did my *oli*, you know, the *mele kāhea*, the *mele komo*.

I went on top and I made them do their *mele kāhea* and I did my *mele komo* and I asked them to start dancing. So we had with us *kaunaʻoa lei* that I had brought 'cause

Kaua'i no more *kauna'oa*, they have but little bit and hard to get. So I brought this *kauna'oa* and I made them put the *kauna'oa* on the back wall of this thing so they put their *kauna'oa* and I, we, had already decided what hula we were going to do and so we started chanting.

I started chanting this hula and all of a sudden I just like, I don't remember anything, I blacked out. I don't know what but I just—the chant was coming out but I certainly know, and even the mothers who was standing off to the side said, that wasn't you chanting. Somebody else was chanting.

Well, what happened was the kids danced this dance we never even know, never ever taught them, and the mothers was taking pictures, was like what's going on, so they was off on the side trying to take pictures of all of this and the kids when it was over, they all started crying. One started crying, the other started crying, they was crying they don't know what happened to them. They don't know what the chant that they did, so I explained to them that I felt that, you know, don't be afraid, was probably something good or something had come inside you and get you da kine, but I had all these crying kids.

The parents was all scared. They were like, kind of like being very defensive to me, like, you know, what you did to them? Or, what did you do wrong? Or, are we supposed to be up there? Or, what this and that? Nobody knew.

Anyway, on the way back we talked about it and I was talking about it and I said it's a good thing, you guys should, like, don't think it's bad and this and that.

It's probably because it's meant to be and somebody, something came inside you and taught this hula and you learned something new even though you never remember exactly how it went but you just did it.

Well, anyway, what happened, too, that I didn't mention, when we left the *pā*, was coming down, when we turned to look at the mountain, da kine, the *kauna'oa lei* that we placed on top, were gone.

So, anyway, we talked about it on the way back and everybody got calm and good and that night we did the performance at the Kaua'i Civic Center and they were so good, they was like, was like wow! They brought the house down and everybody was like yelling 'cause they just were so good, they were perfect, no mistakes, they were so into it. It was a whole different group than what I brought over, it seemed to me.

Anyway, then we all came home and this and that and the mothers developed the pictures. And in the pictures that was the weirdest thing. Two different mothers took pictures, two different cameras. All the pictures were the same in the sense that all the faces, the kids and my face was white. Like white and the hair all standing up like this, straight up from the head in the picture and all you see is a faded thing up against the black cliffs of the *pali*.

So, all you could see was this white glow thing. So, when we saw that we all sat together and everybody cried 'cause was just like wow. So I don't know what it was, I don't understand it, I don't. I'm not *ma'a* to that kine stuff but I know that it truly, there was something that happened. And I know I will always remember that experience.

Akoni Akana is widely known in Hawai'i as a *kumu hula* and cultural resource director on the Po'okela staff of Maui's Ka'anapali Beach Hotel. He is president of Friends of Moku'ula, a nonprofit agency dedicated to restoration and preservation of the private island palace of King Kamehameha III in Lahaina, Maui. Akana still gets chicken skin when he recalls that day on Kaua'i. "There's something else going on over there," he says. "Ghosts of Hula Past" originally appeared as an oral history in *Nā Mo'olelo 'Ōkala: Eerie Stories from Hawai'i,* a senior honors thesis by Jean Kent Campbell.

On Moloka'i's forbidding
north shore, deep in the remote
Wailau Valley on an unusually
still tropical night when nothing,
not even a palm frond stirred, two
young women discover . . .

Things Go Bump in the Night

Whenit happened, we hadn't been asleep very long, but we were definitely both asleep.

My friend Lynda and I were staying in our camp in Wailau Valley on the island of Moloka'i. It was the mid-seventies and my husband, Bill, and I were among a handful of back-to-the-earth folks some called hippies who lived in this majestic, abandoned wilderness once the domain of ancient Hawaiians.

If you have ever been to the north shore of Moloka'i, you know it is entirely uninhabited except for occasional campers and fishermen. Other than for three months in the summer when boats can approach the shore, the only way into the valley is a day's hike over the Wailau Trail from Mapulehu on the East End.

Every visitor to Wailau feels its power. During our years in the prehistoric valley one small experience after another began to impart the understanding that a mountain, or a river, or a seaside cliff could have its own personality. Not only that, but we began to develop intimate relationships with seemingly inanimate features of geography. The valley itself felt like a nurturing mother to me, but the hillside above our camp had a more sinister, menacing quality. There were stories of a woman in old Hawaiian times who would sit up there and watch the ocean for her husband to come home, but he never did. Once when I was all alone at night, I thought I heard a mournful howl coming from that hillside. Many amazing things happened during our time in that magical place, but only once did an event occur for which there was no possible explanation.

Bill had gone on a supply run, and Lynda and I were all alone. We were sleeping on the bamboo floor of our tree-house, which was built into the hala trees on a low bluff overlooking the black sand beach. Lying on the floor between us was the six-foot-long, five-inch-thick washed-in rudder that served as our kitchen table, so we were perhaps four feet away from each other. We were sleeping head to toe—Lynda's feet were pointing mauka, toward the valley, and mine were pointed makai, toward the ocean. Later, when Lynda retold the incident to her kumu hula, she was told that maybe the reason something strange happened was that her feet were pointed toward a heiau.

It's possible that we were the only people in the whole valley; certainly there was not another person within a couple of miles of our camp. The towering valley walls and the endless ocean separated us from the nearest road, the nearest electric light. In the dark of the moon, only starlight broke the blackness. Nothing stirred, there was absolutely no wind, even the ocean was quiet. The night was totally silent.

From a deep sleep I suddenly felt a sharp whack on my right ankle and I sat up and said, "What was that?!" Lynda said, "Something hit my head!" I replied, "No, something hit my foot!"

We were both wide awake now! We got up and lit the kerosene lantern. As I said, no wind rustled the trees, there was not a sound around the camp. Overhead, the roof was intact, nothing could have fallen from above. About three feet from where Lynda's head had lain was a heavy book that had been in our book box. Out over the edge of the bamboo deck, on the ground below, near where my feet had been, nestled a small hala fruit. Whatever hit me felt like it could have been that bumpy, hard fruit. But how could these objects have struck us simultaneously, four or five feet apart, in the middle of a windless night? Where had they come from? Was there someone there? No, there was no way any person could have hit us both at the same moment and then made no sound getting away from the treehouse.

The funny thing is, we weren't really frightened, although our eyes were very wide as we looked at each other and wondered exactly what had just happened. We had the sense that it was something mischievous, not threatening. Were the stories of menehune true? Who or what was with us here in the middle of nowhere? All we knew was that there was no earthly explanation for what we had just experienced, and to this day it is a mystery.

Pam Soderberg and her husband, Bill Dunn, moved to Hawai'i from the mainland in 1974 and settled on Moloka'i during their first month in the Islands. They lived there full time for twelve years, of which three and a half were in a wilderness camp in the north shore Wailau Valley. Even after moving to O'ahu, they held on to their house in the plantation town of Maunaloa for ten more years, unwilling to let go of the Friendly Isle. They now live in Kailua on O'ahu.

*T*ravelers to Hawai'i seldom look beyond the luau or hula show for the cultural roots of these islands, but if they do they sometimes encounter more than they expect. When Lee Quarnstrom, an inquiring West Coast journalist, went in search of the "real" Hawai'i on O'ahu's North Shore, he found something very unusual at Pu'uomahuka, a sacrificial *heiau* overlooking Waimea Bay, where three of Capt. George Vancouver's men from the *Daedalus* were offered in sacrifice in 1794. On that altar of ancient rocks where tiny symbolic sacrifices still appear today, he encountered an old Hawaiian woman about to be displaced by "progress" and discovered that from the distant shadows of centuries past he was being . . .

Watched

Wittingly or by accident, nearly all those who visit the Hawaiian Islands find themselves in the presence of the supernatural. For many tourists, the *mana* of a sacred place or an individual of great power goes unrecognized, written off, perhaps, as the effect of the swaying palms or of one too many rum drinks. Objects such as a feathered cloak at the Bishop Museum are observed as mere curiosities. The plaque telling the story of the Wizard Stones next to the police station at Kūhiō Beach goes unread, or causes chuckles about the superstitious natives. *Heiau*, ancient altars, are overlooked or noted only as piles of rocks. *Kūpuna* who know secrets about the gods or the universe seem like old coots or crones. Dancers following traditions passed down for centuries become "hula-hula girls," and musicians and chanters seem dissonant if they stray far from the "Hawaiian Wedding Song" and that famous little grass shack at Kealakekua, Hawai'i.

Yet those things and people and places and songs and dances are as likely as not to be manifestations of something divine. Generally, this recognition of the sacred in the shadows of Waikīkī or at the edge of the road or on the little stage at the mezzanine bar adds another level of pleasure to the encounter.

Sometimes, though, it can be downright spooky.

I have felt great dread at the beach just south of Ka'ena Point, the legendary leaping-off spot for the souls of the departed of O'ahu on their final journeys to *pō*, the primeval place of darkness. My sense of dread had nothing to do with the Avis car-rental warnings against leaving cameras on the back seats of cars parked at remote beaches. I never feel threatened in Hawai'i, no matter how far I am off the beaten path.

There are two obscure *heiau* on a ridge above Wailuku, the county seat on Maui. On one visit to the old altars I almost saw, from the corner of my eye, a troop of helmeted Hawaiian warriors defending their sacred stronghold with clubs and spears against an onslaught of enemies from another island. I looked around and saw no one, of course.

At the top of the Pali above Honolulu you can almost hear the voices of the defenders of O'ahu, killed by soldiers of Kamehameha the Great in a bloody battle at the edge of the precipice, screaming up the sheer windward mountain-side.

And who, familiar with Hawaiian customs and beliefs, doesn't wonder, seriously wonder, whether that woman or that girl at the edge of the Big Island road wasn't Madame Pele?

I have felt the *mana* many times at many places on these most beautiful of islands. But only once have I felt my skin crawl.

On O'ahu's North Shore, not far from the entrance to the park at Waimea Falls, a winding road leads up past the Foodland market from the Kamehameha Highway. From below, it seems to meander up to some luxurious homes where rich people enjoy spectacular views out across the most famous stretch of surf anywhere in the world.

Many years ago, on a lark, I turned up that curvy lane and continued until I saw a small sign with an arrow pointing into the jungle and notifying visitors this was the entrance to Puʻuomahuka, a *heiau* that is part of the state park system.

What led me off the highway or what made me turn onto the rutted dirt road into the park I do not know. The driveway turned into little more than a trail, pitted with homes, lined at a couple of places with abandoned automobiles inexplicably smashed until they were almost flat. I wondered at what enormous engine—or, more likely, what powerful hatred of mainland machinery—had crushed those once proud and shiny American sedans.

Rounding a sharp curve, I was forced to slam on my brakes: ahead of me on the narrow road two men in rangers' uniforms were trying to restrain an old woman, who was shouting and pointing to a nearby shack that had just about been leveled by a bulldozer.

The old woman tore herself free and rushed up to my car.

"I am the *kahuna* of this *heiau*," she yelled at me. "They are tearing down my house. Help me, help me!"

To make a longer story short, the state was widening the entrance to Puʻuomahuka and was taking out this *kahuna's*—was she really a *kahuna?*—rude little home. I told her I would tell her story to a newspaperman I knew in Honolulu. She smiled at me and quietly and calmly walked away from the rangers. She had asked for help; she had gotten it.

Actually, even though I relayed her story to the reporter, it never got told in print until now. Perhaps this very story you're reading is what that wrinkled old woman wanted and was expecting.

I drove on up the hill and soon came out of the trees to find myself at a small parking lot next to the *heiau*, one of the largest in the islands. From the altar, which dates back to antiquity, I had the most amazing view I've ever seen: the

ocean, Waimea Bay below, sandy beaches, green fields to
the right, steep, dark mountains to my back, the grassy banks
of Waimea Stream far below.

Out there in the ocean, I later learned, was where Capt.
George Vancouver anchored his ship two centuries ago so a
party of his sailors could go ashore to fill barrels with fresh
water from the stream. And on the very spot where I stood,
the Hawaiians who lived nearby and worshipped at that
place took the lives of the unlucky seamen as a sacrifice to
their deities.

And even today, I realized as I walked around the altar,
feeling the huge stones placed there before white men ever
touched this archipelago, this *heiau* is a center of worship.
Everywhere, I saw, believers had placed little tokens of
devotion, substitutes for the enemies who were once sacrificed at this spot. On the walls of this altar there were
smooth stones wrapped and tied in leaves of the sacred ti
plant; there were coins hidden in remote crevices; there were
flowers and spoiling pieces of fruit and colorful bits of rib-
bons purposefully left here and there.

Yet who had left them? I wondered. Is this place still in
use as it was historically? Do Hawaiians come here to pray?
At certain times of the year only? At night? Every night? Or
by day?

And suddenly, alone there on that magnificent plateau
with its sweeping panorama, I felt the hairs on the back of
my neck stiffen.

I was being watched!

Trying to seem cool, I turned, and kept turning. There
was no one there; at least there was no one visible. I peered
into the trees and bushes at the back of the clearing. Was
someone there? If so, how many? Were they locals who'd
found me trespassing on their holy ground or were they
watchers from another time, perhaps from the time when

this island was ruled by chiefs not yet beholden to the great Kamehameha?

I got back in my rental car and drove away. The ancient *kahuna*, sitting now at the side of the road as the 'dozer finished demolishing her cabin, smiled at me as I hurried past.

Now you know, she told me with her eyes.

Now you are a part of this.

Lee Quarnstrom, a reporter and columnist for the *San Jose Mercury News*, lives in Santa Cruz, California, a spot he believes is the easternmost point in the Hawaiian Islands. He is a frequent visitor to Hawai'i.

From black sand beach to its red dirt canyon rim, the Big Island's lush green Waipi'o Valley sweeps back six miles between 2,000-foot-high cliffs laced by 1,200-foot-high Hi'ilawe Falls. The "valley of kings," once the political and religious center of Hawai'i, is steeped in myth and legend (here Māui was dashed against the rocks by Kanaloa) and full of the bones of old Hawaiian chiefs, maybe even those of Līloa and Lono. When helicopter pilots spot new caves in the sheer cliffs, they alert the Bishop Museum, which sends out an intrepid archaeologist who sometimes discovers that something beyond bones remains to be seen in . . .

Cliffside Burial Caves of Waipi'o Valley

Waipi'o is a delightful place to explore. You can hike down and up. For backpackers, the trail up the opposite side of the valley just back of the beach goes atop the cliff to Waimanu Valley. This all-day hike takes some preparation. Please, let someone know where you are and the days you will be gone, and arrange with them to notify the Fire Department Rescue Squad if you do not return on time. The rescue squad logs more calls here than anywhere else.

And now for my Waipi'o story. One week about thirty-five years ago we had a medium-sized earthquake centered near Waipi'o Valley. Several landslides occurred in the valley and along the shore-side cliffs. The next day a helicopter pilot flying along the cliffs reported that a landslide had opened the mouth of a formerly sealed cave. The pilot reported to Bishop Museum in Honolulu that he looked into the mouth of the cave and saw a large stack of human bones. Hawaiiana researchers at the museum keep a master map of the islands with all the important finds marked on it. This cave was something new. They sent over an archaeologist to investigate.

A cliffside burial cave. The problem was getting to the cave. The opening was midway up the face of a 1,200-foot cliff with the ocean crashing at its base. The museum solicited my help and that of a helicopter. The helicopter transported six of us to the cliff's edge along with rope and pulleys. As the helicopter hovered beyond the cave's opening, so we could judge its location from above, we lowered the archaeologist down. He had a sketch book and a flashlight. Several hours later he tugged on the rope to signal that he was finished and wanted to be hauled up.

It's one thing to let someone down on a rope, but quite another to haul him back up. It took us all the rest of the day to haul him up foot by foot. The researcher concluded that the site was a burial cave of a major chief, who along with his warriors had died in battle before white men came to Hawaiʻi. The chief was laid out on a *heiau* of rocks within the cave. Bodies of his warriors had been stacked at the opening of the cave.

The interesting part was how the burials had been accomplished in such an impossible place high on the face of a perpendicular cliff. Found inside the mouth of the cave was a tree trunk with a hole bored through one end. Apparently, skilled climbers had scaled the cliff, then hauled the tree trunk up on a line. They anchored one end of the tree in the cave, and sticking the other end out in the air, used it as a boom to haul up the bodies.

There was also a spooky mystery about the cave. The archaeologist could not complete his investigation. He said his flashlight stopped functioning when he tried to go deeper into the cave.

Gordon Morse, author of children's books and travel guides, including *My Owhyhee*, from which this story is excerpted, operated a Big Island adventure camping outfit for twenty years. Raised on Molokaʻi, educated at Boston University, he wrote for the *Honolulu Advertiser* before becoming a Mauna Kea ski guide and Big Island outfitter. He and his wife, Joann, an artist and book illustrator, live in Volcano, in the historic Lyman missionary house, now a bed-and-breakfast.

Kapu

*T*he island of Lāna'i is little
explored, its gold sand beaches
seldom tracked by human foot-
prints. The island's deep valleys
hold no great interest for well-
heeled sophisticates who come
by jet from distant cities and
cling to the two tony resort
hotels, soaking up the
incongruous luxury on one of
Hawai'i's last true wilderness
islands. It may be a good thing
few dare to venture beyond the
borders of the resorts, for Lāna'i
is a haunted island, as novelist
Steve Heller discovered when he
borrowed a key from the Lāna'i
Company and unlocked the gate
to sacred, forbidden Maunalei, a
green cleft in the red dirt island
he came to know, too well,
as . . .

The Valley of Ghosts

The world of pre-Christian Hawai'i was a world inhabited by spirits of every kind. But only one island was known as the Island of Ghosts: the island of Lāna'i. According to many a legend and story, its only humanoid inhabitants were man-eating spirits controlled by the sorceress Pahulu. Hawaiians avoided Lāna'i until the fifteenth century A.D., when Kaululā'au, the mischievous son of Ka'akalaneo, the King of Maui, was banished to Lāna'i for a series of destructive pranks. The banishment was regarded as a death sentence because for more than five hundred years, no human being had stayed overnight on Lāna'i—and lived until the following dawn. Nevertheless, with the help of his *'aumakua* (guardian spirit) the brave and clever prince of Maui was able to trick and kill all of the ghosts of Lāna'i and make the island safe for human habitation.

Today it is said that the only ghosts on Lāna'i are those the visitor brings with him. I discovered the truth of this saying a few summers ago when the Hawai'i Literary Arts Council invited me to read my fiction at the old Lāna'i Lodge, at that time still the only hotel on the island. As a frequent visitor to Lāna'i and longtime student of its history, I had previously visited most of the island's sacred and culturally significant sites, such as Kaunolū (the God's Landing and the favorite summer residence of Kamehameha the Great), the ancient fishponds at Naha on the leeward coast, and Polihua Beach, where the fishing god 'Ai'ai introduced the green sea turtle to Hawai'i by dropping a small stone on the white sand and chanting a prayer to his parents Kū'ulakai and Hinapukui'a. But there was one place on Lāna'i I had never been: the sacred, forbidden valley of Maunalei.

Maunalei is actually a deep green gulch carved into the windward side of three-thousand-foot Mount Lāna'ihale. Narrower and not quite as steep as Waipi'o on the Big Island and Kalalau on Kaua'i, the valley of Maunalei is nevertheless perhaps even more dramatic. According to legend, the volcano goddess Pele often visited Maunalei to gather *'ie'ie* vines, whose roots were perfect for weaving baskets. The steep sides of the valley are still marked by stone terraces built by taro farmers. At the mouth of the valley a Hawaiian village once thrived, supported by the fresh clean water of Maunalei Stream, which once flowed all the way to the sea.

Today the valley is fenced off near its mouth to keep the curious from disturbing traces of native Hawaiian culture, as well as from contaminating the island's primary source of fresh water. On my third and final day on Lāna'i I received permission from the Lāna'i Company to enter the forbidden valley and hike up it as far as my weary legs would carry me.

Using the key the Company gave me, I unlocked the chain fence at the mouth of the valley and drove my rented Jeep up a sandy rutted path through *kiawe* and ironwood trees. After a minute or two the trail began to rise, and suddenly I emerged from the *kiawe*. The sky opened blue above me between the walls of the gulch. Maunalei is more than half a mile wide at this point near its mouth, and the stony gray-green walls slope at forty-five-degree angles on each side. As I drove inland, the walls rose higher and more steeply until they become sheer green cliffs, cutting a deeper and narrower groove in the massive mountain. Maunalei and all its tributaries are marked by narrow waterfalls that send moisture raked from passing clouds cascading down cliffs hundreds of feet high into the stream that flows at times all the way to the sea. Maunalei literally means "wreath mountain," and from the floor of the valley one can easily see why. Clouds are snared by the jagged head peaks of the gulch, creating mist. When the light is right, rainbows arc from cliff to cliff above the waterfalls. The head of the valley is almost always in shadow; clouds and the steep mountainsides block the sun. The hidden head of the valley, the most remote and mysterious place on the island, was my destination.

"Maunalei a place of great *kapu*," a Lāna'i man once told me. "*Kapu*," like many Hawaiian words, is a complex term. It can mean many things: forbidden, sacred, consecrated, special, filled with spirits. Maunalei is all these things, and more—a place of history and legend. Somewhere up on the cliffs near the head of the gulch is Ho'okio Ridge, a fortification where in 1778 Kahekili, the king of both Maui and Lāna'i, was defeated in battle by Kalaniopu'u, King of Hawai'i. Fighting on the side of Kalaniopu'u was Kamehameha, who would one day unite all the islands under his rule. The invaders hurled sling stones at the warriors defending the ridge, and cut off their water supply. In the end the defenders were slaughtered.

After the island fell to Kalaniopu'u, his troops remained for a time. The island had too little food to support both the army and the residents, and in the famine that followed many more perished. Although the evil cannibalistic ghosts of Lāna'i had been destroyed by Kaululā'au centuries earlier, the spirits of all who died on Lāna'i as a result of Kalaniopu'u's invasion are said to dwell in the upper forest and the even higher, shadowed mossy cliffs of the gulch. Maunalei is consecrated with the blood of the dead.

After about a mile and a half of twisting ruts, I rounded a hillside curve. Through the V-shaped opening before me loomed the tall jagged cliffs of the valley's head, its serrated green peaks rising like the spires of a giant natural cathedral. But I was still more than a mile from my ultimate destination. I parked the Jeep at the pumping station at the edge of the green wall of the upper forest. With only an improvised walking stick to protect me, I found a narrow trail and pushed into the forest.

Inside was another world: a forest cavern with a ceiling of green and a floor of black volcanic stone and mashed leaves. The first thing I noticed was the hush. The caressing breeze, the salty breath of the sea I had taken for granted in the open areas of the valley did not penetrate the wood, and the sounds it brought to my ears moment by moment—birds warbling, leaves rustling—vanished with the sky. But the forest was not silent. Inside the wooded cavern every noise is sharp and distinct: the crunch of stones, the snap of twigs beneath my feet, the pitter and shush of water over rock. Each sound carried through the trees. Not an echo: a lingering resonance, like a lone note held on a piano. The depth and weight of my movements were amplified; instinctively I fell into a reverent silence, proceeding in slow, almost mincing steps. The valley narrowed noticeably as I advanced, crossing and recrossing the narrow stream. Tiny fruit balls crunched beneath my feet, and ferns clutched at my pant legs. I paused a moment beside a sixty-foot waterfall on the side of the gulch, then pressed ahead until the encroaching flora forced me to crawl over slick stones in the center of the stream.

Then all at once the roof opened. I emerged from the upper forest and found myself in the bottom of a giant ravine, ten times as high as it was wide: the deepest cleft in the mountain. On each side of me, slick green mossy walls rose a thousand feet or more. Somewhere above the mountain, thunder rumbled, and I shivered as the air grew suddenly colder. As gray clouds gathered overhead, forming a roof above the ravine, I felt stifled, edgy, as if the sides of the ravine might collapse on me at any moment.

I remember feeling this way only once before, a decade earlier in 1978: the morning my wife, Mary, and I drove our VW campmobile up the Big Thompson Canyon in Colorado, the day of the tragic flash flood. At the canyon's narrowest points, the winding walls of the Big Thompson are almost vertical and cannot be climbed by anyone but a professional. Nevertheless, log cabins dotted the banks of every other bend in the river. On the morning Mary and I snaked our way up toward Estes Park, a rolling ceiling of gray cloud poured down the canyon, shutting off the sun. I remember thinking that if the clouds opened and spilled their contents, there would be no way out, no way to escape the resulting flood. The water would simply sweep away everything in its path. Don't be a worrier, I chided myself as I drove. And besides, there was nothing I could do.

We drove all the way to Gunnison that day, and didn't learn of the flood until we turned on the TV in our room at the Best Western that evening. It turned out we had missed the storm and flood by one hour. I no longer remember how many people perished in a matter of minutes that day. I remember only the images of destruction: cars twisted and smashed like toys against sheer cliffs; rectangular-shaped grooves in bare slick earth, marking the spots where log cabins had once stood; bodies half-buried in ripples of mud. In one shot, a single hand reached up out of smooth brown glaze and stretched upward, as if there were something in the empty air above to grab onto.

I was lost in this memory when all at once the ceiling of clouds above me collapsed. For an instant, I didn't know where I was: in Maunalei or the Big Thompson. In seconds, the steep walls around me vanished, and I stood enveloped in billowing gray. Then it began to rain. The stream, merely a trickle moments earlier, began to surge around my ankles, then my calves. There was no escape. Whatever spirits inhabited this place would claim me now, if they wished. I could do nothing but stand and wait.

Then, as swiftly as it had come, the gray cloud passed. On each side of me, vertical cliffs sparkled green in a thinning mist. I stood, soaked and shivering in the returning light, and drew a deep breath.

Ahead of me, at the head of the gulch, a distant waterfall, created by the cloudburst, tumbled in a spindly white ribbon from a notch in the cliffs. For a few moments I just stood there and stared at it. Somewhere above and beyond the waterfall lay Hoʻokio Ridge, and the final mysteries of Maunalei. Someday I may hike the final steps up the valley and confront them.

But not this day. On this day, I turned back.

Steve Heller's first book of short stories, *The Man Who Drank a Thousand Beers*, has been called "a Hawaiian *Winesburg, Ohio.*" Currently Professor of English and Chair of the Creative Writing Program at Kansas State University, Heller recently served as Distinguished Visiting Professor of Creative Writing at the University of Hawaiʻi-Mānoa, during which time he began work on a new novel called *Private Island*, tracing the history of Lānaʻi. "The Valley of Ghosts" describes the experience that inspired a short story, originally published in *Hayden's Ferry Review*, called "The Ghost Killer." Other stories relating to Lānaʻi are forthcoming in *Nebraska Review* and *Bamboo Ridge: The Hawaiʻi Writers Quarterly*.

Naturalist Rob Pacheco makes his living exploring the forests and trails of the Big Island of Hawaiʻi. He's a practical outdoorsman, not one to believe in the supernatural, yet one day after a long, grueling hike across lava beds, he experienced a strange feeling that he shouldn't have gone to . . .

A Place Called Kapaoʻo

Anyone who spends any time outdoors in Hawaiʻi comes across a place where there's something going on. You know, something heavy. There's a lot of stuff out there nobody can explain. Weird stuff. I know a geologist who hiked two hours to a remote place, turned around and found himself face to face with an old woman with white hair. Some say it's Madame Pele, but I don't know.

I always experience heavy chicken skin in lava tubes. There's something about being in a deep, dark place and not knowing where it goes or what lies ahead. You know that we've got the longest lava tube cave in the world? On the Big Island. Kazumura Cave. It's thirty-four miles long. It's behind locked gates over fourteen miles of bad Jeep road in totally isolated volcanic country. Want to go? I just got permission to go there. You climb down on a traverse line like a spider in the dark. That's real chicken skin.

I've never really experienced anything, you know, real scary, but one place in particular comes immediately to mind. There's this place called Kapaoʻo, it's down on the western outskirts of the park. It's just typical Hawaiian archaeological ruins, a pile of rocks and other stuff. The park service is really weird about it; they act like it's not really there. "Well, ahh, yeah, it's just a place," they say, and, "Why do you want to go there?"

They obviously don't want anybody to go there. You can't find it on maps or anything. It's not even in the book of ancient places. Supposed to be a temple to Kū Uli, the fish god, lots of sacrifices there.

Even the Hawaiians don't go there, and those who know, they don't tell anybody about it. They don't want anybody to go there. I heard about it—I can't say who told me—but I decided to go and check it out, see what all the fuss was about. That was about 1992, shortly after I arrived in Hawai'i.

It was a long, hot, windy hike in, and real voggy. The vog stuck in the place, and once we got there it was just real windy and voggy and awful.

Nothing happened. Except this weird feeling. You just get a real foreboding. I felt like I shouldn't be there (laughs nervously). I don't know what it was, and I can't explain the feeling, but there definitely was power in the rocks. I just got the feeling like, "What are you doing here, *haole* boy?" We were not supposed to be there. It could have been ancient *kapu*, I suppose, I don't know. I'll probably never know. We left, and I never went back. I only get that feeling now inside a lava tube or whenever I'm trespassing.

Rob Pacheco is founder of Hawaii Forest and Trail, an eco-adventure outfit on the Big Island of Hawai'i. A naturalist guide, he goes by day into Pu'u 'Ō'ō rain forest to spot endangered native birds; by night he leads hikers to see Kīlauea's red-hot lava flow into the Pacific. On his treks he offers details on the island's geology, biology, botany, history and ancient myths.

H-3 Freeway Collapse a Mystery

RICK CARROLL

Four 120-foot-long, 40-ton concrete girders supporting Hawai'i's nearly completed H-3 freeway collapsed for no apparent reason in O'ahu's Hālawa Valley on July 27, 1996, injuring four carpenters.

Work on the freeway stopped while puzzled safety engineers probed the wreckage, which Hawaiians blamed on violations of sacred *kapu*.

The freeway goes through a valley considered by Hawaiians to be sacred. Freeway construction disrupted an ancient *luakini heiau*, where Hawaiian women once observed rites.

"It makes me nervous—especially nervous of the unknown," Patrick Stinson, vice-president of Kiewit Pacific Co., the general contractor, told the *Honolulu Advertiser* in a Page One banner story on Tuesday, July 30, 1996.

The mishap is the latest in a series of mysterious accidents, two of them fatal, that have occurred on the project.

"We want a Hawaiian priest to bless that site," Walter Kupau of the Hawai'i Carpenters Union said. "A lot of times people don't believe in spirits and stuff, and a lot of time I don't. But I believe sometimes strange things happen."

"They have to be careful when they go into an area where it's filled with Hawaiian sites," Mahealani Cypher, a Hawaiian researcher, told the *Advertiser*. "They have been very disrespectful to these sites. They go right in and bulldoze it before they have had proper consultation."

More than three decades in construction, the $1.37 billion, 16.1-mile H-3 interstate freeway is the most expensive ever built in the world. It connects Pearl Harbor with Kaneohe Marine Corps Base Hawaii and is scheduled to open sometime in 1997.

The project, which had been blessed repeatedly since construction began in the 1960s under the Statehood Act, will receive yet another blessing, the contractor said.

1n Hawai'i, when modern science probes old ways, something inexplicable can happen. What happened to Phil Helfrich when he went to Maui in search of the mysterious cause of a deadly fish poison is a classic example.

Limu Make o Hāna

For three decades, as late as the 1970s, we were looking into the cause of Ciguatera fish poisoning. Some fish would be poisonous and others would not. It would wax and wane. So there was a lot of mystery about it, a lot of tales about what caused it and so forth. Since then, we've discovered what causes it, and most of it can be explained, but back then it was a still a great mystery.

In the process of looking for a source of the toxin, in other words something that manufactured it, we explored all areas. And in looking through the literature, in Pukui and Elbert's *Hawaiian Dictionary* we found something called *limu make o Hāna,* which was defined as "the deadly *limu* or seaweed of Hāna."

We learned that it had traditionally been found in a single tidepool on the coast of Maui beyond the town of Hāna. We determined where the tidepool was and decided to go investigate.

Now the Hawaiians used to put this seaweed on the tips of their spears and do in their enemies, and it was reportedly very deadly poison. We got some samples of this from a friend who lived in the area, who was very secretive about the whole thing. The sample included a coelenterate (a sea anemone) and some algae. We tested the alcohol that it was in and it was highly toxic, one of the most highly toxic substances we've ever tested.

So because of that we went to try to find the tidepool and investigate first hand. I went with a graduate student on New Year's Eve, the afternoon of New Year's Eve, and I forget the year exactly, but it was about 1959 or 1960.

We went down to Hāna, to this location on the coast where the road was about almost a mile above the coastline. And in the process of going down to the coast, we encountered a local man living in a small house on this property who asked us why we were there. We told him about our search for the origin of Ciguatera, and explained what we were doing, or hoping to do, and he told us that the area was *kapu*, that it was sacred and that we shouldn't go to the tidepool.

We told him that we felt we had to in the interest of science and that this kind of research is often very important to cure diseases like cancer and so forth. And he kept saying that the area was *kapu*. He said he couldn't stop us from going to the tidepool, but he did say that if we went into the area something bad would happen to us.

About three o'clock that afternoon we went to the tidepool. We collected the material, or what we thought was the material, and came back to discover that what we collected was the algae, which was the wrong thing.

When we got back up the cliff, the old man looked at what we collected and said, "Well, you collected the wrong thing, that's not *limu make o Hāna*, but that's okay, something bad is still going to happen to you."

It was about 4:30 in the afternoon. We got back to the road and drove back to Spreckelsville in central Maui where we were staying. The phone was ringing as I entered the house.

It was news, bad news; the laboratory on Coconut Island had been completely destroyed by fire. And I mean completely. It almost burned down the adjacent buildings. Things like the refrigerator were melted down to little blobs of metal. So of course all my files and manuscripts and, you know, my total office was destroyed.

So before I left to go back to O'ahu I asked my colleague, this grad student, to go back to the tidepool and collect the coelenterate.

And he did so. Once again he encountered this man.

The grad student was pretty nervous about the whole thing, but he went back to the tidepool.

He had some cuts on his feet and he waded around in the pool collecting the coelenterate. He didn't realize that this toxin, if it came in contact with body tissue other than skin, could have a very detrimental effect.

On his way back to central Maui with the specimen, he became very ill, was hospitalized and almost died.

One more thing I should tell you: In the laboratory, once we got it going again, we found that *limu make o Hāna* contains one of the most potent bio-toxins known to man. So the Hawaiians were on to something.

Normally, when we make a test we inject laboratory mice, and it takes thirty to forty minutes for symptoms to manifest. When I made the initial test the results were so dramatic I thought I'd made a mistake. Before I could remove the needle from the mouse, it was dead. A total lethal injection. That led us to go on and experiment further.

The Hawaiian community wasn't at all cooperative. They didn't even want to talk about it. It was through a cousin of my wife's who lives on Maui that we made a connection over there, who just sort of told us on the sly that, well, you know, *limu make o Hāna* is somewhere below such and such a point on the road.

Phil Helfrich is the retired director emeritus of the University of Hawai'i Marine Biology Laboratory on Coconut Island in Kāne'ohe Bay. A marine biologist in Hawai'i since 1953, Helfrich served with the Rockefeller Foundation as director of the International Center for Living Aquatic Resources Management in Manila. He is now writing the history of Coconut Island with Dr. Paul Christiaan Klieger of the Bishop Museum Anthropology Department with a grant from the Edwin Pauley Foundation of Los Angeles. *"Limu Make o Hāna"* originally appeared as an oral history in *Nā Mo'olelo 'Ōkala: Eerie Stories from Hawai'i,* a senior honors thesis by Jean Kent Campbell.

Ghosts

When Arnie Palmer and Jack Nicklaus built championship golf courses in Hawai'i, they had no idea Hawaiian ghosts would be a major handicap or that chicken skin is par for the course. And if an elderly Hawaiian gentleman starts talking to you on Kaua'i's Poipū Course, heed his words.

Ghostly Golf

There have been times that I'd have sworn my golf swing was haunted by an ancient Irishman named Mulligan, but until recently I'd never put golf and ghost in the same thought.

Then things started to, well, happen.

And all of a sudden, certain things started making sense.

Like the time that Craig Stadler made a four-putt bogey after driving the green of the par-4 13th hole of the Kapalua Bay Course during the Lincoln-Mercury Kapalua International. Stadler, one of the stars of the Professional Golfers Association Tour and a former Masters champion, smacked his tee shot 300 yards to within 40 feet of the pin. Thinking eagle and no worse than birdie, Stadler putted short, then long, then long, and at last barely lipped in the fourth putt.

This kind of stuff just doesn't happen to PGA stars. So for years I chalked it up to Just One of Those Weird Deals That Happen Sometimes.

But then not long ago I was back at Kapalua, researching a story on the Maui resort's certification as an Audubon Society Cooperative Sanctuary, and started talking with a couple of Bay Course greenskeepers, Kimo Kiakona and Arnile Libunao. As they tell it:

It was still dark that morning as they put out pins and tee markers on the 13th and 14th holes.

"I seen 'em first, this white thing," said Arnile. "At first I thought a water pipe had busted, or maybe the sprinklers were on. It looked like water shooting up, except there was no sound."

He immediately called Kiakona, a native Hawaiian.

"I saw this white thing, like walking toward me, taking steps. But when I turned the headlights of the cart on it, there was nothing there," Kiakona said. What was it? Nobody knows.

Now Hawaiian culture is rich with ghost stories, and Kiakona said his elders have talked about seeing ghosts and that this one fit their description.

"I know it was one ghost," he said.

In the pro shop, they weren't sure if it was Casper the Friendly Ghost or if they should call Ghostbusters.

At about the same time, on the other side of the West Maui Mountains at Sandalwood, a Hawaiian warrior clad in loincloth and gourd helmet was suddenly appearing to golfers, materializing at the edge of trees lining the seventh hole à la Shoeless Joe Jackson in *Field of Dreams*. While the story has been widely repeated on Maui, neither professional Fran Cipro nor anyone on his staff has ever seen the apparition.

"I heard one story about eight guys seeing this thing and leaving in such a hurry they forgot their clubs and carts out on the course," says Cipro. "That's just never happened."

If you believe that spirits linger about graveyards, then there certainly is a chance that ghosts get into golf. The 13th hole of the Klipper Course at the Kāne'ohe Marine base runs between the sea and a sandy hill that is an ancient burial ground for Hawaiian royalty. The second and sixth holes of O'ahu's municipal Kahuku course skirt an old cemetery. The third and fourth holes at the Bay Course run past a large, grassy mound that is believed to be home to the largest burial ground in the Hawaiian Islands. The dune that runs between the sea and the 17th and 18th holes at Poipū Bay, Kaua'i, is home to old bones. The course also includes two *heiau*, or ancient temples.

And then there are the "birthstones" located in a thicket of dense jungle above the 15th hole at Ko'olau Golf Course at the windward base of the Ko'olau Mountains. The stones are actually boulders, large enough to fill a room, carved in the exact likeness of the towering mountains above.

Five hundred years ago and more, Hawaiian women went there to give birth, and as they awaited their time they carved the stones. I took a Hawaiian *kahuna* friend, Kawena Young of Hilo, there, and as she walked among the stones running her hands a few inches from the surface of the stones, the hair on the back of her arms stood straight up.

"There is heavy *mana* here," she said. Then, holding her hands above one rock in particular, she said: "There's so much *mana*, here, it tingles, it almost hurts."

Later, she chanted and thanked the spirits for allowing us to be there and asked for their blessing. Now Ko'olau is officially the toughest course in the United States and probably in the world, so there's no other reason than Kawena's chant to explain why I have always played that hole well and with luck.

Twice, I've had severely sliced tee shots bounce out of the jungle on the right of the hole and onto the fairway. Another time, an approach shot struck way too strong, hit a tree at the back of the green, and dropped into the grass, from where I chipped in for birdie. Heavy *mana*, indeed.

But that's not the heaviest *mana* story that I've heard about on a golf course. That distinction goes to a series of stories told to me while I was covering the PGA Grand Slam at Poipū Bay for *Golf Week* magazine. Greg Norman, Nick Price, Ernie Els and Jose-Marie Olazabal were about to tee off on the second day of the 36-hole competition. I waited beside the first green when an older Hawaiian gentleman walked up and started chatting. He wore the arm band and carried the "Quiet Please" paddle of official course marshals. He said that he had helped build the Poipū course as well as several others around the islands as a bulldozer operator.

"Every time I have to break the *'āina* (the land) I always tell the spirits 'I'm sorry, but this is how I make my living,'" he said.

Sometimes, the spirits listen, sometimes they don't.

"On this course, three times, we had funny things happen, things you can't explain. "There's two *heiau* on the back nine, one on the shore by 16 and 17, the other inland by 10. Three times, on pretty flat ground, we had Caterpillars tip over. There's no way to explain it but it happened."

He continued:

"I spent three years in the hospital after one accident on Lāna'i. Lots of funny things happened there, too. One time I was working on the course there and there was a sacred site. My Cat flipped over on me. I almost died. Years went by, I wasn't healing, so finally I called a *kahuna* and she came and I got better."

He added that friends of his had worked on the H-3 Freeway on O'ahu.

"They kept moving a big rock and when they come back the next day, it's there again. That rock wanted to be there. They finally hauled it away. The guy who had it moved was from the mainland. The next day, he was walking where the rock had been and a small branch fell out of a tree overhead and fell down and poked out his eye."

By this time the PGA Grand Slam foursome was approaching the first green, and I had to get to work. I thanked the gentleman for his stories and asked his name.

"Only if you don't use it," he said. I promised and he gave me his name and his son's phone number where he could be reached.

When Rick Carroll asked me to contribute to this book, I wanted to confirm some details of the old gentleman's story, so I phoned the son on Kaua'i. He was flabbergasted.

"When did you talk with my dad?"

"November of 1994," I told him.

"That's impossible," he whispered. "He died in 1993."

Author, columnist, golfer Don Chapman is editor of *Midweek*, Hawai'i's largest-circulation newspaper. A former *San Jose Mercury News* reporter, Chapman came to Hawai'i in the 1970s to surf and play golf. He wrote a daily column for the *Honolulu Advertiser* for 13 years, until 1992, when he took early retirement to play every golf course in Hawai'i. He now writes about golf for various local and national magazines and newspapers. He is the author of *Boys of Winter: The Story of the Hawai'i Winter Baseball League*.

A fter two decades of searching cemeteries, Nanette Purnell has only one real-life chicken skin story. It's a good one. While researching graves on O'ahu's Wai'anae coast, she agreed to meet a man named Wayne Davis who offered to show her . . .

Old Hawaiian Graveyards

We made a date to meet on a Sunday morning at eight o'clock at Tanouye's, the landmark drive-in on the leeward side. He described himself and I described myself. He said he was a big Hawaiian guy. So on a Sunday morning at eight o'clock I drove up and saw a big Hawaiian guy by himself at the outdoor seating area at Tanouye's.

"Hi, I'm Nanette Purnell. Are you Wayne Davis?"

He said he was and I sat down and started talking story, just chatting you know about this and that.

And then we went driving around in my car for three hours and we visited about twelve different graveyards, many I had never seen before—in the backs of valleys, and really out-of-the-way places. He was terrific; he really knew where to find the old Hawaiian graveyards.

We did this for three hours and I got back to Tanouye's and dropped him off.

The next day I was writing a thank-you note and I got a phone call. I picked it up and this man's voice said, "Nanette, this is Wayne Davis."

"Oh, Wayne," I said, "thank you again for taking me around. I really enjoyed it and I learned a lot."

And he said, "What are you talking about?" And then he said, "Where were you yesterday?"

"Wayne," I said, "Are you trying to pull my leg?" I

thought he was making a joke. All of a sudden it hit me, and I started getting chicken skin on my arms, and I said, "Wait a minute. I'm confused. Wayne, did you go with me yesterday?"

He said, "No, I went there and waited for more than an hour and nobody showed up."

Then the hair on my neck stood up. I literally got chicken skin up and down my spine and I got scared.

"Wayne, don't joke with me, this isn't funny. I went there, at eight o'clock, and met a man who said he was Wayne Davis and he got in my car and he took me to all the graves for three hours."

"Nanette, I don't know how to tell you this, but that wasn't me."

It wasn't funny to me now. "Were you there or not?" I demanded.

"I wasn't there," he said. " I called because I just wanted to find out what happened to you."

He said he arrived late for our appointment and waited, but I never showed up so he went home.

I still didn't know who took me around, and it really bothered me, so about a month later I talked to this *kupuna* and told her the story and she told me to think of it this way, that maybe the ancestors were calling on me, sort of like an *'aumakua*.

"The old Hawaiians wanted you to know where they are," she said. After that I felt good about it.

Several months later, at a function, I saw a man with a name tag that read "Hi, I'm Wayne Davis," and I introduced myself. It was the real Wayne Davis, all right, at least he said he was.

And, are you ready for this? He wasn't the same one who took me around the old graveyards.

Nanette Purnell is Hawai'i's foremost authority on graveyards. Founder of The Cemetery Research Project, Purnell spent 20 years scouring 300 cemeteries to learn who's buried where in Hawai'i. Her findings are in three journals now in Hawai'i state libraries. "Cemeteries are full of stories," Purnell says, "like the man who shares a common plot with three ex-wives in King Street Catholic Cemetery." A guest speaker at conferences of cemeteryologists in Boston, Los Angeles, and Hawai'i, Purnell has appeared on "The MacNeil-Lehrer Report" and "The CBS Evening News with Dan Rather." She is now writing the history of O'ahu Cemetery and leading walking tours to historic graveyards. She lives in Kailua. A version of this story first appeared in *Midweek*.

The bloody battle for Oʻahu by Kamehameha the Great in 1795 came back to life one night not so long ago when a Honolulu bus driver paused on the Pali Highway at the end of his shift and heard warriors "fighting, yelling, and dying." A young boy recalls this vivid story often told to him in . . .

My Grandfather's Ghosts

Well, I'm twelve years old and I happen to believe in ghosts and I'll tell you why: It's all because of my grandfather (who, by the way, is a big, brave, strong man). He's six foot two and I don't think he was ever afraid of ghosts. Until one night, long ago.

When I was four or five my mother told me the story about my grandfather and the ghosts of the Pali Highway, a story that didn't make sense then, but later, when I was six or seven, it really started to register and come into focus. This is how the story goes:

My grandfather was a bus driver and he was driving the Old Pali Road route one night, in spring or summer around 1956. He had already dropped off all his passengers and he was the only one on the bus.

It was just before midnight and he had turned off the bus, relaxing and waiting for his last run to start back down the hill to Honolulu. He was waiting for midnight so he could end his shift. All the bus drivers did this to keep on schedule.

Suddenly, he heard a lot of noise. It sounded like some kind of fighting was going on. He heard yelling and it got louder and closer. Next, he heard the clashing of what sounded like wood spears and clubs and men screaming in agony. It was like a war. Bam! bam!

As the sound came closer and closer my grandfather's bus started to shake like somebody mad was pushing it around, rocking it, and the trees were getting blown all over the place.

It's always windy up there, but this wasn't a normal gust of wind. This was something else. Then, all the sound and commotion came so close to my grandfather he began to believe that men were really fighting, yelling and dying.

When it sounded too real, he decided to get out of there as fast as he could and zoomed back to the bus depot. He was really frightened by it all. Just sitting up there even at daytime, to me, it's kind of scary with the wind and all.

My grandfather went to the dispatcher and told him what he had heard and felt up there on the Pali.

"We can put you on another route if you want," the dispatcher told my grandfather. And he agreed on the spot.

Next morning, he was told by some of the other drivers that they, too, had heard these noises in the past and asked to be transferred.

The Old Pali Highway route that my grandfather and others drove in those days was the same way that King Kamehameha had taken when he came to fight Chief Kalanikupule of O'ahu.

The famous Battle of Nu'uanu happened in April 1795, when Kamehameha's warriors fought Kalanikupule's. Some of Kalanikupule's warriors were driven over the *pali* (cliff) at the end of this valley.

Now, it seems that at certain times, usually around midnight, people traveling alone on this Nu'uanu route have experienced hearing these spirits fighting their way up the Old Pali Road.

Whenever I travel that road, today, I always keep my eyes peeled for the ghosts of the warriors of Kamehameha and Kalanikupule. I'm sure they are there. So is my grandfather. I wouldn't take a hundred dollars to spend the night up there alone. So keep your eyes peeled, too, when you cross the Pali alone at midnight.

Son of a Windward O'ahu sailmaker and a *kumu hula*, Nicholas Love grew up hearing stories his Hawaiian grandfather told. A promising storyteller in his own right, Love, who is twelve, already has won numerous creative writing awards. He attends Lanikai Elementary School, where he is a seventh grader. "My Grandfather's Ghosts" is his first published article.

When a University of Hawai'i English instructor joined an archaeological dig on Moloka'i in the early '70s, she met the dead of Hālawa Valley in broad daylight and soon became so surrounded by ghosts she made . . .

An Informal Census of Moloka'i Ghosts

Pūko'o itself, on Moloka'i's East End, had three ghosts. A woman in white walked on the highway. A dead Chinaman swung from the rafters of the old stone house across the road that had once been owned by the famous von Tempski family. And a creature lived in the big *haole koa* thicket: woman by day, giant squid by night, in the old days she used to creep down to the pens by the beach to eat the pigs. These creatures came out on nights when the moon and stars were blotted out by clouds. Since even by my time there were no more pigs at Pūko'o, only the bulldozed hotel site, how the squid woman and the others continued to manage was no longer clear.

One East End family allowed a brother-in-law who was not a blood relation to clean out their well. A few nights later the mermaid paid the brother-in-law a visit. The mermaid was very pretty. She had white hair and smoked a cigar. She liked men. The brother-in-law woke up to find her pulling the blanket off his bed. He jumped up and ran out of the room. The mermaid drifted next door, where she tried to suffocate the baby. The whole family got on their knees reciting prayers and obscenities. After the old grandmother had said the Lord's Prayer backward ten times in Hawaiian, the mermaid finally went away.

Moloka'i must have been one of the last places in the

islands you could hear people speak in ordinary conversation—as opposed to the Madame Pele stuff handed out either to impress tourists or as deliberate revivalism—of the *moʻo,* the giant lizard of Hawaiian mythology. According to East End legend, the little lagoon west of Pūkoʻo that was being dredged for a hotel had a resident *moʻo* already responsible for the death of one man and the injury of another when a bulldozer tipped over. It was a great example of the old forces of imagination mobilized against the new, how the supernatural functions as an allegory for the collision of cultures. And guess who won? Even though it managed to cause some damage, in the long run the *moʻo* did not stop the hotel. . . .

Mainly, I remember how the word was spoken, all by itself, with a slightly exaggerated widening of the eyes, in a semihokey lowered voice—*"Moʻo!"*—embodying all the paradoxes of simultaneous belief and skepticism that torment those sentenced to life imprisonment in the Grand Canyon of fault lines between cultures.

Then you had the *heiau,* the very-old-days place of worship. The first I ever visited in the Islands was ʻIliʻiliʻōpae, halfway between Kaunakakai and Pūkoʻo. In a jungle of overgrown java plum and guava behind a cow pasture a huge platform of mildewed green lava rock reared suddenly above the trees. . . . The rocks stopped fifteen feet up and what you had, impressive enough in its own way, just like the fishhooks and bone needles instead of skulls carved out of crystal or the king's ruby, was a huge flat platform about the size of a basketball court, with indentations still visible for the long vanished "god sticks," the carved wooden statues of the gods with protruding tabs at their feet that were inserted in these holes somewhat like the plastic chess pieces on miniature portable boards. Big ceremonial *heiau* like this one would have needed a passel of attendant priests. Walking on this broad, surprisingly even surface just above the level of the treetops, I was struck by how neatly the eggplant-size lava rock was graded into smaller and smaller stones, their interstices filled in with coral rubble for easy walking just like in the old house platforms. A *heiau*, I realized, was nothing more than an enormous house platform for the gods.

Hālawa Valley itself had the remains of two smaller, older *heiau* that stood sentinel on opposite sides of the valley mouth commanding a wide view of the ocean and the cliffs. These would have been kin group or fishermen's *heiau*, parish chapels as compared to the regional cathedral.

Though Hālawa's ghosts had ebbed with the receding tide of its full-time occupants, each trail in the valley had once had its own chant to be recited against bad spirits; the famous Twelve Winds of Hālawa were still identified by name. Even in my time a driver who eased his car down the dirt road into the valley could hear his name spoken out loud at the bend where the road crossed an ancient Hawaiian footpath. In the empty tin-roofed houses a mirror fogged, a child cried, a white dog ran down the decrepit hallway.

I met the dead of Hālawa Valley in broad daylight. My first skeleton was huddled under a house platform a little way up the talus slope. As I brushed away loose dirt with a whisk broom the shape sprang out at me: a child crouched in the earth like an ancient bird about to spread its bony orange-stained wings and fly.

We recorded the pathetic remains and covered them with a flannel rag weighed down with lava rocks. When the whole platform had been excavated and photographed, the dirt would be filled in again with the bones remaining *in situ*. This was after all a new era of archaeology, geared to sensitivity to local feelings. Many people on Molokaʻi had either lived in Hālawa Valley themselves or were related to those who had. The municipally illegal custom of burying deceased kin in the backyard was still widespread. Nobody wanted to think his grandfather's skull was going to spend all eternity labeled and numbered on a basement shelf in the Bishop Museum. To the Moloka'i people these remains were Subjects, recent ones, not Objects.

The first year of the Hālawa dig, the archeologist Gil Hendron was sitting in Kane's Bar in Kaunakakai one night having a peaceful beer when a big Hawaiian man came up to him. At first Gil didn't understand what he was mad about.

The man said it again, louder. "You fuck with them bones?"

He was enormous. Gil knew the answer. "No!"

"You fuck with them bones," the man went on in a voice laden with menace—and here the pronoun was the surprise, "They come back, bust you up!"

"Coming back" was fairly standard practice for the dead of Moloka'i. By all accounts its ghostly population was as large and vocal as the living one. Dead relations swarmed like bees around the households of the East End. You couldn't keep them away, it seemed; they pressed in all around you clamoring their requests trivial and profound. All day long in the trenches the kids regaled me with these stories; in the evening visitors like Mrs. Akina and others picked up the thread. Many East Enders came back, they told me, and for all kinds of reason. One boy's grandfather came back because the cows from Murphy's Pu'u o Hoku ranch were trampling his grave. A mother came back to her three daughters as a loud wind in the night, but they were never able to determine her wishes.

In one of the precious camp paperbacks, a dog-eared copy of Claude Levi-Strauss's *Tristes Tropiques*, I read the great French anthropologist's account of an Amazon tribe's beliefs about the afterlife: "The souls of Nambukwara men are incarnated, after death, in jaguars; but the souls of women and children vanish into the air and no more is heard or seen of them."

If nothing else, my informal census of the Moloka'i ghosts serves as dramatic rebuttal of the Nambukwara spiritual hierarchy. On the East End, at any rate, as many women and children came back as men.

Victoria Nelson, an instructor of English at the University of Hawai'i from 1969-1973, is the author of *My Time in Hawaii: A Polynesian Memoir,* from which this account is excerpted.

Everyone likes to look at old
pictures in the family album,
recalling happy days of
small-kid time, summer days at
the beach, first day of school,
summer camps and birthdays
with Grandma and Grandpa,
high school and college
graduation, family weddings,
and the first baby luau.
Sometimes, old pictures stir up
memories best left forgotten.
When strange things began to
happen in his family home, Ed
Chang found the source of the
problem under the house
in a box full of . . .

Old Pictures

This happened in my family. I guess it was back in the '50s, the early '50s, '51, '52, something like that. My uncles and my mom have old pictures. You know, real eggshell-looking, oblong pictures of her grandfolks. They're all dead. And my mom didn't like to put pictures of people who were dead in our house. So what we did was put them under the house. In big old suitcases, the old, old type. They were all stored under the house. After they were there about, I'd say about a year, every night my mom would experience something, like the house move or something opening up underneath the house or some kind of noises.

So my dad and older brothers would go out there and check and they would see the trunk move. The lid would move. They thought it was just wind or something. But then my older sister, Clara, she started getting dreams of old people. They would come in to see her and talk to her. She would wake up crying and she would tell my mother, "I seen this old lady with one eye. She's got long black-and-white hair and she's on crutches." My mother knows that her grandmother looked just like that. She had one eye, she had crutches and had always protected her long hair.

It got worse, where my sister started seeing more people. Like my grandpa's mother. Several people came in the dream, and my sister described them. My sister never did see the pictures.

My mom went under the house and got all the pictures. They had old newspapers covering all of them individually. Now they were all torn apart like rats got in there. And shuffled around. They weren't in the order she put them. She started getting scared. She went to the minister, my mom did. She talked to the minister about this. It was getting worse because everybody in the house was afraid. Even I was afraid. Nobody wanted to walk out of the house at night in the dark.

Down Wai'anae is real dark anyway. Anyway, the minister came over to the house and he blessed the whole house, grounds and everything. He took the pictures, and one of the pictures just crumbled in his hands when he was praying, you know like, "Get rid of the devil," or something, and the picture crumbled in his hand like it was shivering in his hand. And we all were there, we all saw. You know, he was just holding it and praying over it and it just busted in his hand.

After that night that the minister came over to pray, my dad decided that we sell the place, never knowing that as long as we had the pictures with us that was still going to happen. We bought another place up in the valley, Mākaha Valley Road. It was a two-and-a-half-acre lot, and we stored the pictures under our Quonset hut. And it did happen again. I experienced it, my sister experienced it, my mother, my father, my uncle. We all saw some vision of our grandfolks. We had to get rid of the pictures.

So my mom took all the pictures to church and the minister took them and burned them. He burned them by himself. My mom just left everything with him. He burned the pictures in his back yard in a fifty-five-gallon drum.

A couple of Sundays later, he didn't want to bring it up,

but he did. He said he had to tell my mother because he couldn't hold the secret in. He said when he burned the pictures he saw all different kind of colors come out of the pictures and he heard cries. He said it actually happened to him.

It never happened to us again so we don't have any of our grandfolks' pictures no more. I don't know why all that happened but it did.

Ed Chang worked for many years as a night security guard at Makapuʻu, where he encountered plenty of unusual experiences. Nothing he found on the night beat, however, proved to be as intense as what happened to his own family in "Old Pictures," which originally appeared as an oral history in *Nā Moʻolelo ʻŌkala: Eerie Stories from Hawaiʻi,* a senior honors thesis by Jean Kent Campbell.

Grandma said they were angels, but they weren't. They came down from the West Maui Mountains at night. They walked *through* the house. They entered the nursery. They stood above the crib where Louise Aloy's newborn baby girl slept so peacefully in her crib. Who were they? Why were they there? What did they want? And what did the mother do when she found out that . . .

They Miss the Baby

I live in Kahului, and I've been living there now since 1986. But it was only when my daughter was born that I decided to turn my sewing and storage room into a nursery. So I put the crib along the wall, and an extra bed and my rocking chair and the dresser changing table. Oh, it was a real pretty, real nice nursery. Real nice to move into, you know.

But, anyway, the baby stayed in there, and there were nights when I went to nurse and rock her and I just went to sleep there. But there was just something about that room. Didn't hear anything from the landlord, maybe because she didn't believe. But you know your hair would stand up. I would be nursing the baby, rocking. It was like somebody behind you was watching, but yet not knowing whether it was anything or, you know, you just have that feeling, that intuition or premonition.

Then as the baby grew older, we would hear her laughing. And you know, my mother said, "The angels play with the child," so you just shrug it off. She would like goo goo ga ga ga, making like conversation with somebody. As she grew older you wave your hand like this in front of her face and she'd be staring. And she still does it now and she's three and a half.

'Kay, so anyway one night I was real tired. Instead of

going to my room I slept in her room on the bed. Then it was the dark night, starless night, and I don't know what came out, but somebody had walked across me. Somebody or something, then hoo, couldn't get up. Heavy, I thought I was going die. I was screaming for help. My mouth was open yelling anything I could think of, Hail Mary, Our Father. My mind was going, but heavy, heavy, heavy. I never went back in there to sleep. But I left the baby.

Her two brothers were in the middle room. And they didn't feel anything, except one of my oldest son's classmates. He said every time he passed the baby's room he got the willies. He got the heebee jeebies. Now this is a kid who live up the street, he not with us all the time. He just said, "Ooh, your sister's room give me the willies." But he would go in there and peep on the baby and say she was real cute and stuff.

Well, it had been bothering me since that time it walked across me. So I had called Nalu, you know who Nalu is. Nalu from Lahaina and Peter Kaina, the one from Napili. But anyway somebody gave me somebody's name to come and bless the place and the three of them came.

They walked around my property. Went in the room, out the room, in the driveway, you know they do the little trip, four corners of the house. Then they brought us into the living room and we all congregated and they all prayed and then they all came out and told us a story. And what the two, the older and the younger of the three men had felt was that we were, the house I live in was sitting in the pathway of a tribe. They weren't headhunters, they weren't night marchers. They was just a very, very old Hawaiian tribe. And he said they were coming from the mountains and they went through Briyana's bedroom at an angle. They always stopped by, a few of them stopped by the crib and played with her. So they had grown to love her.

But you see I didn't know that was all going on, so before she was a year old I took her out of that room because she was getting bigger. She would stand up and climb and you know I just didn't want to be leaving her alone so I moved her into my room. But they followed her. Her father felt it. 'Kay, don't ask me why, just one night we were all in the bedroom playing with the baby and stuff and he sensed this lonely, lost despairing spiritual being by the doorway looking in on the baby.

But I never think about anything, I just left it in the back of my mind, but when Nalu them came to tell me the story, without my telling them about that incident, the older one said the tribe was a little bit *huhū* that the baby wasn't there anymore and they wanted to know where the baby went. But they only went through that path. They didn't deviate, it was a no no for them to deviate from the tribe, so they just went that way and when they stepped on me I was in their way, that's where my *pūne'e* was. See they came from the mountain, they passed the crib, played with her, but at an angle they crossed over me and that's when I had them step on me you know, but I didn't know anything, they certainly weren't harming me. It was just one of those things. So I moved the bed around and stuff.

He told me that the tribe even had a scout. It was a man he said he pictured carrying a box and the first thing came to my mind, *auwē*, they are going to put my baby in the box. Then he said, "Oh, wait," then he did this whatever and he says, "No, they're putting it down in your front yard." And the leader, the little guy, the scout puts the box down, the leader stands on it and talks to his people.

So it's very very very heartwarming. It really is after you listen to it. Because then the older of the two Hawaiian men asked the younger one what kind of spirit he felt on my driveway. How come you felt another one on my driveway?

His answer was they had another scout who cleared the area when they went toward the beach for food. So it's kind of a nice story, you know. And now I'm not even afraid. My kids are not. And if anybody feels the willies, we just, "Oh, that's our family passing through." And in fact my son's friend now comes and since we told him the story no big thing now. He can go in and out of that nursery, which since has changed into a little office, baseball card showroom, Boy Scout room, you know, nobody uses it, not because of that, it's Briyana just grew up.

And I welcome them now if they want to know how she is doing. When Briyana is in that area I can still wave my hand in front of her face and she's just giggling away, laughing and talking. She talking to them, I know she is, 'cause she not listening to me and it only lasts not more than thirty seconds then she's right back to herself again. And you know what her famous line is, "But I playing with my friends." Cute, you know. "I have to play with my friends, I gotta say goodbye." Oh so it's just like make-believe, you play with dollies right? Everybody did that. Well for her she has her make-believe friends but I don't think it's make-believe. I think it's really true only she can see them. I can't, but obviously those two Hawaiian men could see 'em or could at least feel 'em, because one, his hair would, you know, really rise.

Louise Aloy is a single parent of three. She works as a purchasing director at Ka'anapali Beach Hotel on Maui. Her daughter is seven now. The Aloy family moved to a new home in Wailuku last summer. Aloy says, "Whenever I see my daughter playing and laughing and giggling with imaginary friends, I'm always grateful she has some great Hawaiian spirits watching over her." "They Miss the Baby" originally appeared as an oral history in *Nā Mo'olelo 'Ōkala: Eerie Stories from Hawai'i,* a senior honors thesis by Jean Kent Campbell.

Animals

When U.S. geophysicists set up a remote observatory on top of 13,679-foot-high Mauna Loa on the Big Island of Hawai'i in 1957 and began a top secret mission to monitor the atmosphere for solar and nuclear radiation for the Atomic Energy Commission, they discovered a more down-to-earth mystery, one that continues to baffle some of the world's best scientists. Perhaps it was only the high altitude, or an optical illusion (although one scientist did take a photograph as proof) and maybe it all had something to do with the Pele legend, but the mystery remains to be solved. Our story takes place on the summit of the world's biggest mountain, where scientists grew confounded by the inexplicable comings and goings of . . .

The White Dog of Mauna Loa

No reminiscence of Mauna Loa Observatory would be complete without mentioning the white dog of Mauna Loa. Much has been told about the mysterious phantom dog that would appear on the mountain to forewarn of a volcanic eruption. Hawaiian legend relates a tale of Pele, who is the fire goddess of the volcanoes on Mauna Loa, and her companion dog, whom she would send as a messenger to alert the people whenever an eruption was imminent.

The white dog was first noticed by the observatory staff during the latter part of 1959. At that time the staff were living on site for up to a week at a time on rotating shifts. Because of this housekeeping, a rubbish dump was soon developed to the west of the observatory. The contention of the staff was that a stray white dog had discovered the dump and foraged it for food. Attempts by the staff to befriend it and later to capture it, no matter how persistent or devious, failed. The dog for some reason would have nothing to do with the observatory staff. Soon the dog disappeared and was presumed to have found its way back to the populated regions of the island. In December 1959, Kīlauea Iki erupted.

To the amazement of the staff the dog reappeared at the observatory several months later and again was spotted intermittently for a month or so and then disappeared. This pattern of appearances and disappearances continued until 1966. Since then, to my knowledge, no one has seen the dog.

Its appearances or disappearances were never regular, and at times it was seen at the summit as well as farther down the access road to the observatory. It would never have anything to do with anyone and whenever pursued would always easily outdistance its pursuers over the rough lava and run to the top of the mountain.

The staff could never determine where it obtained food when it was not at the dump (months at a time) in the desolate environment of the mountain nor why, if it did descend the mountain when it was not seen, it did return to roam the mountaintop for months at a time. This was especially puzzling in view of the fact that the staff sometimes discovered lost hunters' dogs wandering close to the observatory, always in the most pitiful condition. In every case, starvation and exposure to the elements had just about done in these hunters' dogs.

Concerning the belief that the white dog was a messenger of pending eruptions, it is true that it was sighted sometimes before an eruption, but it was also sighted many other times when no eruption occurred.

The dog did create a problem for the staff in that when a staff member would describe the appearance of the dog to visiting scientists or to the public the response would invariably be looks of worry and discomfort or of concern and a fear that this staff member had finally gone stark crazy.

The story of the dog was definitely out of place among scientific endeavors at the observatory, and soon the staff members were hesitant to talk about it to anyone they did not know. To this day the mystery of the white dog is just that—a mystery.

Geophysicist Bernard G. Mendonca joined the Mauna Loa Observatory as a part-time government employee in 1958 while a University of Hawai'i student. He originally helped the U.S. Weather Bureau process analysis from atmospheric monitoring of solar radiation and later, in a classified program, monitored nuclear radiation for the Atomic Energy Commission. He now works at Geophysical Monitoring for Climatic Change in Boulder, Colorado. His account of "The White Dog of Mauna Loa" originally appeared in *Mauna Loa—A Source Book of Historical Eruptions and Exploration, Vol. Three, The Post-Jaggar Years (1940-1991)*, edited by Walther M. Barnard, Dept. of Geosciences, State University of New York College at Fredonia, New York.

1n Hawai'i it is rare for anyone
to see a *pueo*, the endangered
Hawaiian owl. When you
see two, it could be a sign,
but what does it mean
when you see hundreds
and hundreds
of owls in
broad daylight?

When Pueo Gather on Moloka'i

She was an old woman and she was dying. Her family knew she would die soon, probably that afternoon, and they came and stood by her bed.

She kept saying, "My family will come and take me away." Her family members were puzzled by her remarks.

They went outside and sat on the lanai and noticed two owls on nearby fence posts. How odd, they thought, to see two owls in bright daylight. They heard sounds of the woman dying and went inside to attend her death.

Then they came outside and the entire area around the house was covered with owls. There were hundreds and hundreds of owls. They were making kind of a barking sound and they stayed for a while and then they all left.

Anonymous lives on O'ahu. Credit, he says, should go to the *kanaka maoli* who told him this story. "When *Pueo* Gather on Moloka'i" originally appeared as an oral history in *Nā Mo'olelo 'Ōkala: Eerie Stories from Hawai'i,* a senior honors thesis by Jean Kent Campbell.

On the Hāna coast of Maui stand the ruins of Pi'ilani Hale, the largest royal residence on Maui. Here King Pi'ilani, the first king of Maui, lived in a 60-acre royal community on a large bluff overlooking the Pacific until his death around 1500 AD. For generations Hawaiians have been warned by their elders to stay away from the *heiau*, a massive stone temple—174 meters long and 89 meters wide—which probably served as a *luakini*, or war *heiau*, and a place of human sacrifice. Now a national historic landmark, Pi'ilani Hale is often visited by students on field trips who sometimes meet . . .

The Great Gray Cat of Pi'ilani

We were visiting Pi'ilani Hale Heiau on Maui and this was my first trip there. There were ten of us. Some of the kids were kind of running and jumping and fooling around and I told them, "Look, we're visiting a *heiau*, just kind of calm down and don't act so crazy." They felt kind of contrite and we continued on our way and I showed them a house site of Pi'ilani.

Suddenly, out of nowhere this big, huge gray cat just appeared and walked straight over to me. I'm not very fond of cats, and vice versa, but this cat just kind of comes right up to me and I petted it and I have never seen eyes like this in a cat.

The whole person of this cat was very strange. Everybody had this same feeling about the cat. The cat just started walking away, then it would look around like, "Well, come on."

We went with the cat and we got to the *heiau* and I didn't know how to get up to the *heiau* because it's this thirty-foot-high wall. It's surrounded by breadfruit trees, and the cat just kind of walked up on top of this house.

We followed the cat 'cause it waited up there for us, and then it walked over to this ramp that we didn't see at first. It walked right up the ramp onto the top of the *heiau* and it walked straight up to the main altar of the *heiau*, which was covered with brush, and we kept following the cat.

At that time I didn't know it, but it was the main altar. The cat kind of walked around it as if to say, "Here you are."

Everybody started talking about this strange behavior. Wasn't that kind of weird that this cat showed up out of nowhere? And led us to the main altar? Where we were now standing. Then, everyone looked around. "Where's the cat?" No cat. It was gone.

Anonymous lives on O'ahu. Credit, he says, should go to the *kanaka maoli* who told him this story. "The Great Gray Cat of Pi'ilani" originally appeared as an oral history in *Nā Mo'olelo 'Ōkala: Eerie Stories from Hawai'i,* a senior honors thesis by Jean Kent Campbell.

Haunted Places

The Bishop Museum is an imposing edifice, forbidding like a mortuary, solid as a small-town bank. Few seeing it for the first time doubt the 1889 Victorian building could be anything but a grand old museum, an enormous repository of cultural artifacts. There are, I am told, 20 million acquisitions from Hawai'i and the Pacific—ancestral relics, religious figures, spirit idols, feather capes, war clubs, skulls and bones of dearly departed Hawaiians, the inevitable dust of a once proud Polynesian kingdom. Sometimes I think of the gray lava stone building as a kind of mausoleum of *mana*, chock full of captive spirits. When I see all the fishhooks carved out of the human bones of defeated warriors I can't help but wonder if spirits still haunt this place. As I long suspected, when the doors close and night starts to fall, strange things begin to happen . . .

At the Bishop After Hours

I found her in Archives, a tiny Asian woman who sat at a desk covered with manuscripts, surrounded by volumes of history, translating what appeared to be Hawaiian words heavy with *'okina* and *kahakō* into plain English.

I had come to the Bishop suspecting that the repository of the greatest collection of Hawai'i and Pacific artifacts in the world must teem with ghostly stories. Who has not gazed upon the royal capes of King Kalākaua and imagined the Monarchy coming to life in Hawaiian Hall at the stroke of midnight?

To confirm my suspicions I sought out this Japanese woman with the unlikely *haole* name of Pat Bacon who is something of an artifact herself. She is a child of the museum, the *hānai* daughter of Mary Kawena Pukui, the famed Hawaiian translator and author of the *Hawaiian Dictionary, Hawaii Place Names,* and thousands of other manuscripts.

"I practically grew up at the museum," Mrs. Bacon told me, and, in fact, she arrived as a small child to sit at her mother's side. "My first job here was in 1939; then I got married and quit. I came back in 1959 and," she said with a laugh, "I'm still here." She seemed both proud of and surprised at her tenure. I figured her time at the Bishop amounted to seven of the eleven decades the museum has been in business. If there were skeletons in the closet, this woman would know where they were, but she seemed reluctant. She wanted to know more about my project. I told her it was to be a collection of true, inexplicable stories of events experienced by skeptics.

"What do you mean by 'skeptics'?" she asked in her precise, library-soft voice, one eyebrow arched.

"Those who doubt or do not believe," I replied.

"I believe," she said evenly. "I am not a skeptic. I was raised in a Hawaiian household. We learned to deal with both today and yesterday. We were raised Christian, but we were told we could not doubt those kinds of things. They did exist."

What kinds of things, I asked. And who are "they"?

"Those things." She laughed nervously. "You know, whoever or whomever, or whatever. It's hard to explain," she said. I think I knew what she meant.

"We grew up showing respect to things we couldn't understand or explain," she said. "The older Hawaiians knew all the rituals and *kapu*, but we were not taught. We were taught to respect the old ways, but they were not for us at this time."

Had she ever been frightened by strange events in the museum? I had in mind a desolate wandering ghost hovering over a skull on a shelf in Anthropology searching for lost kin. Before she could answer, a thin man with a beard dropped a tray of slides behind her. The clatter startled us. We laughed and she continued.

"My encounters have not been such that I have been afraid of anything. I feel quite safe. But there are others who have had scary things happen. It was years ago:

"A botanist here during the '30s, who came to work at night with her dog, heard footsteps going into the room next door. She knew her dog could see something, because its hackles would rise. But nobody was there.

"Sometimes you hear noises but you can't prove what it is. I've never been here at midnight, but I've been here at 10 p.m. and I never saw anything," she said, "but there are others who have had experiences, who have been frightened.

"Years ago, in the '60s," she said, in a voice so soft I had to draw my chair closer, "a night watchman used to see this Hawaiian woman in a light gown with silvery hair walk across the courtyard to climb up and sit in Queen Lili'uokalani's carriage," she said, and paused. "And her feet did not touch the ground.

"She never said anything to him and he never said anything to this apparition. He saw her a few times at certain times of the year, but I don't remember when."

He quit to work elsewhere. The royal carriage later was moved inside and placed on the second floor of Hawaiian Hall. The night visitor has not been seen since. Maybe she was only trying to get the queen's carriage moved indoors for safekeeping.

"In the late '50s, in Anthropology," she said, "I would double lock the door at night and go home and in the morning one lock would be open. But nothing was moved or disturbed."

She smiled.

I told her that Dr. Yosihiko Sinoto, the museum's own legendary Pacific archaeologist, had told me that some nights when researchers would stay late working all alone in Anthropology, they would hear typing in the room next door, get up, go and look and, of course, nobody was there.

She smiled again.

"Sometimes when I worked late I would open the windows and sit down again and they would be closed. Okay, I'd say, and I'd close them up and go home but I wasn't frightened. I always feel quite safe here. That's how they were talking to me. They wanted me to go home," she said. "So I did."

There are signs, you know, warnings, to heed. She told me about one old, almost forgotten *kapu*:

"If you are out at night and all alone and come upon a sweet smell like *pīkake* or gardenia, and there's nothing there, it's a warning. Get out, get away from the area. Leave it alone and go away. You leave it alone and they leave you alone."

I've never thought gardenias, a flower I usually associate with Billie Holiday or Polynesian women with a certain style, could be capable of issuing *kapu* warnings in Hawai'i, but Mary Kawena Pukui's *hānai* daughter spoke with such conviction it was difficult not to believe her.

Of all the incidents at the Bishop, the most spectacular, she said, involved a bloody death on the stones of Waha'ula *heiau*, which archaeologist John F. G. Stokes brought back from the Big Island of Hawai'i in the 1930s for a museum exhibit.

For those unfamiliar with Waha'ula *heiau*, it was built in A.D. 1250, and was in use until the early 19th century. It was the last temple destroyed by chiefs who banned ancient rites the year before Christian missionaries arrived in 1820.

One of the bloodiest sacrificial temples in all of Hawai'i (its name means "red or sore mouth"), the *heiau* had many ghosts, including one made famous in the 1915 edition of William D. Westervelt's *Hawaiian Legends of Ghosts and Ghost Gods*. "The Ghost of Waha'ula Temple" tells the story of the son of the high chief of Ka'ū, who was killed by the Mū, or body-catchers, and sacrificed on the altar. His ghost managed to return, recover his bones, and flee to the spirit world.

Not so lucky was a young Hawaiian man who worked at the Bishop in the '30s while the Waha'ula *heiau* model was on public exhibit.

"His mother had a dream that warned of danger to her son and she asked him not to go to work, because something would happen. He didn't believe her, but those who were working up there on the roof saw something, they don't know what," Mrs. Bacon recalled.

He fell though the skylight to his death on the *heiau* made from the stones of Waha'ula.

"Old people at that time said the *heiau* had been consecrated by claiming its first sacrifice," she said.

"Mr. Stokes was the one who cleaned up all the blood there," she said, leaving the implication that he never should have removed the stones from the *heiau* in the first place.

The intrinsic power of the stones was further demonstrated in 1989 when red-hot molten lava from Kīlauea volcano destroyed the $1.2 million National Park Visitor Center, ran up to the very edge of the *heiau's* sacred stones— and stopped. I made a note to take a look at those stones, which she thought might still be in the garden of the courtyard.

Since many objects in the museum hail from all over the Pacific, I wondered if perhaps a Papua New Guinea spirit mask, or maybe a moai kava kava wood carving from Rapa Nui ever got out of line and stirred excitement. I imagined an anarchy of artifacts, a revolt of relics hissing and spewing ancient curses.

"Oh, there have been a few things," she said, "but by and large, I think they—whatever it is that is in and around here—have really liked being here, because nothing sinister has happened. So we must be okay."

The bones of two old Hawaiian chiefs, however, did walk out of the museum one night not long ago, probably on the shoulders of burglars who looted the museum of what is known as the *kā'ai*, two woven sennit caskets that contained the 500-year-old bones of Hawaiian chiefs Līloa and his great-grandson, Lonoikamakahiki. The bones had been held in trust by the museum for 76 years and, despite double locks and round-the-clock security, vanished without a clue on the night of February 24, 1994.

Considered sacred by Hawaiians and obviously priceless, they are, or were, historically significant because in and among the human remains were cloth and metal objects that may have pre-dated Capt. James Cook's 1778 arrival in Hawai'i. And since the weave of the sennit is like no other found in Polynesia, their origin has always posed a mystery to archaeologists.

"They were so beautiful," she said. "You know those are the only ones that exist in the world. The workmanship was really beautiful."

The *kā'ai* were brought to the museum by Prince Jonah Kūhiō Kalanianaole in 1918 for safekeeping until a suitable burial chamber could be erected at the Royal Mausoleum in O'ahu's Nu'uanu Valley. Held in a locked cabinet in the collection storage area of Anthropology, the *kā'ai* were last seen at the museum February 17, 1994, when the museum was fumigated for termites. To this day the burglary remains one of Hawai'i's great unsolved mysteries.

Did she have any clue to their disappearance? "I haven't the foggiest," she said, folding her arms across her chest. "I don't even want to know where they are."

I could tell she knew many other stories, but it was time to go, so we said good-bye. She returned to her manuscripts. I went to find the stones that long ago claimed a life at the museum. All I found in the shadowy courtyard was a stone fish idol and the perfectly hewn stone slabs from Kīkī a Ola, Kaua'i's so-called Menehune Ditch. As I searched deeper, the cloying tell-tale fragrance of gardenias began to fill the moist still air. At first I thought it was some cheap perfume worn by a tourist, but I was all alone in the courtyard.

I looked around expecting to see a forgotten lei, perhaps, but there was none and I knew even as the skin on my arms turned to a fine pebble grain that this could only be a sign. I left the museum before doors and windows started opening and closing. I would see the sacrificial stones of Waha'ula another day.

Later, as I thought about my floral caveat and the stories I heard at the Bishop that afternoon, I tried to make sense of it all. Each story it seemed could be explained by logic. Doors and windows opening can be the work of the wind. Footfalls and clacking typewriters are often the product of an overheated imagination. The botanist's dog with raised hackles? A common occurrence. Dogs hear things we don't. I had heard, too, of other sightings of silver-haired Hawaiian women in long flowing white gowns whose feet never touch the ground (Jocelyn Fujii told me her sister saw the woman walking *above* the beach at Hanalei one night). As for the Hawaiian fellow who slipped and fell to his death on the Waha'ula stones? A mere coincidence, don't you think? Or, maybe, power of suggestion.

While the disappearance of the *kā'ai* remains a great mystery, from a detective's point of view it was a textbook case of first-degree burglary. Probably an inside job. I mean 500-year-old bones just don't get up one night and walk out of the museum, do they? Many people I talked to believe the *kā'ai* were spirited out of the museum (you don't suppose by night marchers, do you?) for a proper burial in Waipi'o Valley. Nobody knows, or is saying, where the last earthly remains of the chiefs and a small clue to Hawai'i's own mysterious past now repose.

Bones and stones and old ghosts. The unknown and fear of the unknown almost always cause chicken skin even for skeptics like me. I'm still not altogether comfortable with the idea of invisible gardenias issuing *kapu* warnings. What I do know for sure is this: when I smelled gardenias at the Bishop after hours and my skin began to crawl, I knew that they—whoever they might be—wanted me to go and I did and I was not afraid. In the end it's all in who and what you believe.

RICK CARROLL, author, journalist, travel writer, editor, has written six books on Hawai'i , including *Great Outdoor Adventures of Hawaii.* He is now editing *Travelers' Tales Hawaii,* an anthology of personal discoveries in the Hawaiian Islands.

When a tourist couple wanders into Washington Place, the private residence of Hawai'i's governor, they meet a tall, white-haired gentleman who leads them on a brief tour.

The Ghost of Washington Place

There are many wonderful stories about former Hawai'i governor John Burns. You know he's been gone so long—he died in 1975—but his life and legend are so much alive. Every political season his name comes up as if he's still around, inspiring the next governor or the next leader. It's so strange it's almost eerie.

I don't like to admit it, but I know his spirit is still here. There are times I've felt his presence. I don't ever question it, I just go with it. And who knows? Those apparitions or appearances may very well be true, but I'm not afraid, just glad he's looking over our shoulder.

One of the stories I've often heard is about a tourist couple visiting the State Capitol who wandered into Washington Place (the governor's private residence) accidentally one day. It was in the late '70s or early '80s.

They were alone and looking around when this gentleman, a tall older gentleman, came upon them and showed them around and gave them a running history along the way.

He was very cordial and friendly, and yet he seemed aloof. They described him as being aloof. They didn't know who he was, but he spent, oh, about fifteen minutes on the tour, recalling special features of the house.

Then he excused himself, said he had to take care of something, but to please stay and enjoy the house, and they did. When they got ready to leave Washington Place, a guard found them and asked what they were doing.

"Oh, we were with a tall, white-haired gentleman who was showing us around," they said. And the guard, who was Hawaiian, said, "What tall, white-haired gentleman? (At that time George Ariyoshi was governor, and although he is tall, his hair is jet black.)

"Oh, he was wearing a dark suit," they said. Which is what the governor always wore. And just then they saw a portrait on the wall and pointed to it and said:

"There, that's him."

"No way!" the guard said. "Are you sure that's him?"

"Oh, We're sure it was him," they said. The guard didn't know what to believe, but he didn't have the nerve to tell them who he thought they saw. And they left, never suspecting anything out of the ordinary. The portrait on the wall, of course, was that of Governor Burns. That's how I heard the story.

Emme Tomimbang Burns is a former Honolulu television news reporter and anchor who now is an independent television producer. Her "Emme's Island Moments" is seen regularly on Honolulu television. She is married to Hawai'i State Court Judge James Burns, son of John A. "Jack" Burns, the second governor of Hawai'i, who served three terms from 1962-1974.

The True Story About Morgan's Corner

BURL BURLINGAME

Everyone by now has heard about a place called Morgan's Corner on Nuʻuanu Pali Road. There are a hundred variations of the story, but most involve a dark Pali road, a couple stranded in a car, the disappearance of the man, a steady drip-drip-drip on the car roof, a hook stuck in the door and police who say get out of the car and don't look back . . .

It's a real place. It's where the old Pali road swings back over Nuʻuanu Stream and then straightens out again. It's also where Dr. James Morgan built a villa in the '20s. Morgan's Corner was a well-known slow-down for Kailua commuters in pre-Pali Highway days.

The site comes by its gruesome reputation honestly. In 1948, prison escapees James Majors and John Palakiko invaded the home of Dr. Morgan's neighbor Therese Wilder. They tortured and assaulted her, then trussed up and gagged the 68-year-old woman. She died and Palakiko and Majors were charged with murder and swiftly found guilty.

Sentenced to hang in September 1951, they were being shackled for the long walk to the gallows when Gov. Oren Long stayed the execution. The case polarized Hawaiʻi citizens; many felt the two men were sentenced to die solely because they were not white.

Palakiko and Majors would have been the last people executed in Hawaiʻi. They were paroled in 1963 and had minor brushes with the law afterward. Palakiko died mysteriously and Majors' whereabouts are unknown.

So, if you happen to stop at Morgan's Corner one dark night, listen carefully. Is that the rustle of the wind, or the lonely screams of Therese Wilder?

Burl Burlingame is a historian specializing in 20th-century Pacific history and a feature writer at the *Honolulu Star-Bulletin*. This story originally appeared in the *Star-Bulletin*.

When you rent a house in Hawai'i, landlords usually ask you to provide background information—you know, prior addresses, references and such. They want to know a little something about your personal history. So it seems only fair that a prospective tenant should be able to obtain some historical information on the landlord, perhaps even the house, especially its occupants, past or present, as Mark Allen Howard discovered one night after he rented the corner room in . . .

The House on Ku'ukama Street

The night is calm, the house silent and still. As I lie in my bed asleep I suddenly feel a sense of terror. My eyes flash open, wide and searching. The feeling of terror is stronger and growing. I can't move any part of my body. It's as if I am being held down by an invisible force. Above and to the left of my bed I see a shadowy face staring down at me through my window. My first reaction is to call out to my roommate Willie, asleep in the room next to mine. But I am unable to utter a single word. Terror becomes panic. My heart races in my chest. My breath comes in gasps. I feel helpless and weak. Suddenly, the terrible weight pinning me to my bed is gone. I leap to my feet and look out the window.

The night is calm. The house is silent and still. I see no one outside and then I realize that it's impossible for anyone to look in my window because it's eight feet above the ground. I lie back down on the bed and think it all must have been a bad dream. I close my eyes and quickly drop off into a quiet, easy slumber.

Next morning I awoke surprisingly refreshed with no uneasy feeling. I believed the experience was just a bad dream. I didn't mention the incident to anyone, until now.

The house on Ku'ukama Street is a typical Hawaiian house, open and airy, with a large lanai. I had moved into the corner room of the house six months after arriving in Hawai'i. Dell, the previous tenant in the room, never mentioned anything about strange happenings in the house or my room. Nor had Dave and Willie, the other tenants. They obviously didn't know.

Although the old house seemed solid, nature was bent on destroying it. Termites were eating the house inside and out. On certain nights the termites, flying and crawling everywhere, would swarm inside the house. Every room in the house but mine was affected. I never saw termites or any other insect in my room, but Willie's room, right next to mine, was infested. I thought that was peculiar.

We called an exterminator, who inspected the house and was amazed at what he found. There were signs of termites in every roof joist, except right above my room. It was as if that part of the roof had been treated, because no termites entered the attic above my room. The exterminator was baffled. He couldn't understand why that part of the house would be treated but no others. The termite problem was soon taken care of, but that other odd episode in my room remained a mystery.

A year passed with no unusual happenings in my room.

The night is calm, the house silent and still. My eyes shoot open. A feeling of terror again washes over me. It is happening again. I feel a presence in my room. Again, I can't move. I am held to the bed by some force. I also feel the force is a malevolent one. In my peripheral vision I see the silhouette of a man. He is looking out the window by my bed. He wants to leave the house, but he can't. I want to grab at the shadow, but I can't move a muscle. Panic begins to overtake my senses. Then, as suddenly as the feeling comes on, it disappears. I lie there trying to catch my breath, wondering what the hell just happened to me.

Next morning I told Dave and Willie about the incident. They listened but dismissed it as a nightmare. I would have thought that too, but because of the previous incident and the strange absence of insects I couldn't write off the events as dreams or coincidence.

Another year went by before anything unusual happened again but that encounter was the most intense of all.

The night is calm, the house silent and still. My eyes flash open. The shadowy silhouette stands next to my bed, looking out the window. I sense feelings of extreme loneliness mixed with anger and resentment. This presence wants to leave but cannot.

My body is forced into the mattress of the bed. I am paralyzed physically, but my mind is clear. For the first time the entity seems to recognize that I am present in the room. From the corner of my eye I see him turn slowly toward me and bend over my face. What I see is hard to explain. It is a black-gray mist that seems to ebb and flow within itself. There are no features to speak of, just darkness.

Suddenly my feeling of terror peaks and I hear in my right ear an eerie laugh, a low, guttural chuckle that makes my skin crawl. Instantly the force holding me to the bed vanishes and I leap to my feet on the bed screaming.

"Willie, Willie, there's someone in my room! "Willie came bursting in immediately and turned on the light, his eyes wild with fear.

"What's wrong! What's wrong!" I just stood on the bed panting and sweating, my eyes focused on the window next to my bed. I didn't know what to say. I couldn't explain what happened.

A few days later I went home to visit my family in Florida. While I was gone, some friends of Willie's from

Connecticut visited and one of them, Jim, decided to take my room. He stayed only three nights. Each night he experienced the exact same visitations that I had in ascending order.

The first night Jim awoke frozen in the bed, with someone looking in the upper left windows. The second night he awoke frozen to the bed, with a shadowy silhouette to his right, looking out the window. And the third night he awoke and saw the silhouette to his right; it slowly turned and laughed a low, guttural chuckle that made his skin crawl. Jim spent the rest of the time I was away sleeping in a tent in our back yard.

About a month after I returned from vacation, the owner of the house gave us two weeks notice to vacate the house. She'd decided to move back to Hawai'i and live in the house again. It seemed strange that she wanted us out so quickly. Later I learned that the woman's husband, who built the house, died in what had been my room.

The house on Ku'ukama Street is still there. I drive by every now and then just to look at it. I don't know why, I just do.

Mark Allen Howard was born in Canoga Park, California. He joined the United States Marine Corps in 1982 and was later stationed at Kaneohe Marine Corps Air Station on O'ahu in 1987. He lived on O'ahu for seven years, in Kailua and Kāne'ohe. A recent graduate of the University of South Florida with a B.A. in English and American literature, he currently lives in Palm Harbor, Florida.

Night Marchers

The Marchers of the Night

In the Path of *Huaka'i o Ka Pó*

Night Marchers of Kualoa

Tales about Hawai'i's night marchers always give me chicken skin. And this definitive story by the ultimate source is no exception. As a girl, Mary Pukui heard vivid tales of the night marchers from her Hawaiian mother and relatives on the Big Island of Hawai'i who had encountered them. In 1930, she shared her reminiscences with Hawaiian folklore authority Martha Beckwith. No story I have ever heard or read about Hawai'i's people of the night has ever been told with such authority, contained such explicit detail and, most importantly, offered precautions on how to survive.

The Marchers of the Night

E very Hawaiian has heard of the "Marchers of the Night," *Ka huaka'i o ka Pō.* A few have seen the procession. It is said that such sight is fatal unless one has a relative among the dead to intercede for him. If a man is found stricken by the roadside a white doctor will pronounce the cause as heart failure, but a Hawaiian will think at once of the fatal night march.

The time for the march is between half after seven when the sun has actually set and about two in the morning before the dawn breaks. It may occur on one of the four nights of the gods, on Kū, Akua, Lono, Kāne, or on the nights of Kāloa.

Those who took part in the march were the chiefs and warriors who had died, the *'aumākua,* and the gods, each of whom had their own march.

If (a chief) enjoyed silence in this life his march would be silent save for the creaking of the food calabashes suspended from the carrying-sticks, or of the litter, called *mānele,* if he had not been fond of walking. If a chief had been fond of music, the sound of the drum, nose flute and other instruments was heard as they marched. Sometimes there were no lights borne, at other times there were torches but not so bright as for the gods and the demi-gods. A chief whose face had been sacred, called an *alo-kapu,* so that no man, beast, or bird could pass before him without being killed, must lead the march; even his own warriors might not precede him. If on the contrary his back had been sacred, *akua-kapu,* he must follow in the rear of the procession. A chief who had been well protected in life and who had no rigid *kapu* upon face or back would march between his warriors.

On the marches of the chief a few *'aumākua* would march with them in order to protect their living progeny who might chance to meet them on the road. Sometimes the parade came when a chief lay dying or just dead. It paused before the door for a brief time and then passed on. The family might not notice it, but a neighbor might see it pass and know that the chief had gone with his ancestors who had come for him.

In the march of the *'aumākua* of each district there was music and chanting. The marchers carried candlenut torches which burned brightly even on a rainy night. They might be seen even in broad daylight and were followed by whirlwinds such as come one after another in columns.

They cried *"Kapu-o-moe!"* as a warning to stragglers to get out of the way or to prostrate themselves with closed eyes until the marchers passed. Like the chiefs, they too sometimes came to a dying descendant and took him away with them.

The march of the gods was much longer, more brilliantly lighted and more sacred than that of the chiefs or of the demigods. The torches were brighter and shone red. At the head, at three points within the line and at the rear were carried bigger torches, five being the complete number among Hawaiians, the *"kū a lima."* The gods with the torches walked six abreast, three males and three females. One of the three at the end of the line was Hi'iaka-i-ka-poli-o-Pele, youngest sister of the volcano goddess. The first torch could be seen burning up at Kahuku when the last of the five torches was at Honuʻapo. The only music to be heard on the marches of the gods was the chanting of their names and mighty deeds. The sign that accompanied them was a heavy downpour of rain, with mist, thunder and lightning, or heavy seas. Their route the next day would be strewn with broken boughs or leaves, for the heads of the gods were sacred and nothing should be suspended above them.

If a living person met these marchers it behooved him to get out of the way as quickly as possible, otherwise he might be killed unless he had an ancestor or an *ʻaumakua* in the procession to plead for his life.

If he met a procession of chiefs and had no time to get out of the way, he might take off his clothes and lie face upward, breathing as little as possible. He would hear them cry, "Shame!" as they passed. One would say, "He is dead!" Another would cry, "No he is alive but what a shame for him to lie uncovered!" If he had no time to strip he must sit perfectly still, close his eyes and take his chance.

He was likely to be killed by the guard at the front or at the rear of the line unless saved by one of his ancestors or by an *ʻaumakua*. If he met a procession of gods he must take off all his clothes but his loincloth and sit still with his eyes tightly closed, because no man might look on a god although he might listen to their talk. He would hear the command to strike, then, if he was beloved by one of the gods as a favorite child or namesake, he would hear someone say, "No, he is mine!" and he would be spared by the guards.

Many Hawaiians living today have seen or heard the ghostly marchers. Mrs. Wiggin, Mrs. Pukuʻi's mother, never got in their way, but she has watched them pass from the door of her own mother's house and has heard the Kaʻū people tell of the precautions that must be taken to escape death if one chances to be in their path.

A young man of Kona, Hawai'i, tells the following experience:

> One night just after nightfall, about seven or eight in the evening, he was on his way when of a sudden he saw a long line of marchers in the distance coming toward him. He climbed over a stone wall and sat very still. As they drew near he saw that they walked four abreast and were about seven feet tall nor did their feet touch the ground. One of the marchers stepped out of the line and ran back and forth on the other side of the wall behind where he crouched as if to protect him from the others. As each file passed he heard voices call out "Strike!" and his protector answered, "No! No! He is mine!" No other sounds were to be heard except the call to strike and the creak of a *mānele*. He was not afraid and watched the marchers closely. There were both men and women in the procession. After a long line of marchers four abreast had passed there came the *mānele* bearers, two before and two behind. On the litter sat a very big man whom he guessed at once to be a chief. Following the litter were other marchers walking four abreast. After all had passed, his protector joined his fellows...

In the old days these marchers were common in Ka'ū district, but folk of today know little about them. They used to march and play games practically on the same ground as in life. Hence each island and each district had its own parade and playground along which the dead would march and at which they would assemble.

Mrs. Emma Akana Olmstead tells me that when she was told as a child about the marchers of the night she was afraid, but now that she is older and can herself actually hear them she is no longer terrified. She hears beautiful loud chanting of voices, the high notes of the flute and drumming so loud that it seems beaten upon the side of the house beside her bed. Their voices are so distinct that if she would write music she would be able to set down the notes they sang.

Mary Pukui (1895-1986) began collecting proverbs, riddles and poetic expressions on the Big Island of Hawai'i when she was fifteen. She spoke Hawaiian and English and had a keen eye toward preserving Hawai'i's oral traditions in print, a role not always popular with her own people. In a fifty-year association with the Bishop Museum, Pukui translated thousands of Hawai'i legends, chants, and ghost stories, including "The Night Marchers," published in *Kepelino's Traditions of Hawaii*, edited by Martha Beckwith (Honolulu: Bernice P. Bishop Museum, 1932), reprinted here by permission of the Bishop Museum. She is the principal author of the *Hawaiian Dictionary*, *Place Names of Hawaii*, and *'Ōlelo No'eau*, a treasury of Hawaiian sayings.

Long ago a retreat for *ali'i*, the Big Island's Kohala Coast, now an upscale neighborhood of luxury beach resorts, is laced by old trails still used by night marchers. Clues they are coming are obvious. Fish ponds ripple. Blue water offshore changes color. A hard puff of wind sweeps across 'Alenuihāhā Channel. Hawaiians like Danny Akaka know these signs are natural reminders that a *pō kāne* night lies ahead and you may have to abandon everything. . . .

In the Path of Huaka'i o Ka Pō

Several old trails go through Mauna Lani, and long ago, before the resorts and the hotels, there were five cottages on the property. The people, when they built the houses, maybe they did not know there were old trails at one time, but the trails were used by the *maka'āinana* and the *ali'i*.

On special nights sacred to the gods—*pō kāne* nights, we call them—just before the end of the Hawaiian month, the spirit processions of the deceased chiefs, chiefesses, their priests, some of the warriors and *'aumākua*, or ancestral family guardians, also march along these pathways. They are constantly in use even today. Oh, yes, I know.

On these certain nights they normally go to sacred spots or areas to re-enact the ceremonies they did hundreds and hundreds of years ago. And one spot was this house we stayed in. I didn't really live in the house; I would visit the family who lived there. They were the keepers of the royal fishponds. On certain nights we would be told by the old folks that, "Oh, not good to stay in the house tonight."

We would never question them or ask why. A lot of things of those old days you never dared to question. Okay, we found another place to stay; after that it was fine. I never gave it a second thought, and years later, I came across a person who mentioned to me, "You used to stay down in that haunted house."

"It didn't seem like a haunted house," I said.

"Oh, you weren't there on those nights when the people were marching, and the house would shake and you could hear voices speaking in Hawaiian, some with chants and some with drums."

I never heard someone come around, I said, and then it dawned on me that it must have been them and those were the nights we had to leave. Years later I realized that the house was originally sitting on the trail. So whatever structure was built on the trail they would go through it. That's the real reason the cottage was moved, but I just didn't realize.

The house was one of five that were all termite eaten and in disrepair, so they were moved, taken down and rebuilt on a different spot. The Eva Parker Woods cottage. That's the one by the water, by the fishponds. That was the one the marchers went through. Years after, I found that out. It's a museum now, and I work there as historian at Mauna Lani. Nothing ever happens there now. I always wondered why they moved that house.

Everything in the path of *huaka'i o ka pō* (night marchers) is cleared away now, but there are still spirits in the area. Basically, a lot of these spirits come and visit the area they lived in, and I do tell people about them so when they see them they will not be frightened. Some people who come here do have a sensitivity about what they can see and feel and hear.

You don't have to be Hawaiian to see these spirits; anybody can see, but not everyone can, you know how I mean? Even some Hawaiians like me, I can't see them, but I feel them. You know when the fishponds ripple or the water changes color or there's a sudden breeze across the channel? Those are signs, and even today when I'm so busy with life, I forget until I feel something, a warning that reminds me, oh yes, *pō kāne* nights are coming.

This is a mild story. There are some that I'm very careful not to tell the guests because it might drive them off.

Some guests think it's kind of strange, these stories about the past, but I just tell them, you know we had generations of people living here before us. They may not be here physically now, but this is still home for them.

What needs to be done, we have to ask their permission that we might live among them peacefully. We're not here to kick them out or drive the spirits out.

The spirits linked to the past are still here, and if we are sensitive enough we will see them or feel them. So I usually tell people that what needs to be done is to conduct a Hawaiian ceremony that is a cleansing and purifying and basically to ask those spirits to allow us to conduct our daily tasks and live among them here in this area. And if we offend them in any way, to please forgive us. I think that's the best way I know to do it.

Danny "Kaniela" Akaka is cultural resource manager and historian at Mauna Lani Bay Hotel and Resort. A native of Hawai'i, Akaka is a 1971 Kamehameha graduate. He earned a bachelor's degree in Hawaiian Studies at the University of Hawai'i-Mānoa. A world-traveled entertainer, he speaks fluent Hawaiian, leads history tours, and tells tales of old Hawai'i. The father of five, he is the son of U.S. Senator Daniel Akaka.

If you read the daily papers in Honolulu, which keep track of such things, you will discover there are an inordinate number of mysterious auto accidents that occur, a little too often, on Kamehameha Highway near the old and sacred valley of Kualoa. Single-car accidents, head-on accidents, fatal accidents, strange accidents in which the car suddenly leaves the road and the driver later says he swerved to avoid striking something that appeared in the headlights and streaked across the road. Sure, there's a bad curve in the road, but most of the accidents occur on a perfectly straight section of the highway. Nobody will come right out and say it, and the Honolulu Police Department just shrugs off the accidents as mere coincidence, but there are many, particularly those who live on O'ahu's windward side and drive the highway, who believe the peculiar accidents are the direct result of collisions with . . .

Night Marchers of Kualoa

When I first started working at Kualoa, which is a park on the windward side of the island of Oʻahu, I was told a story of the *pō kāne*, or night marchers. It was said that the night marchers always come from the burial cave on top of the mountain on the night of Kāne, which can be identified as the 25th night of the month, according to the Hawaiian calendar.

Supposedly, the remains of more than four hundred chiefs are in those caves. In the night of Kāne they descend in a procession. Back before World War II there was a German army officer visiting Kualoa. Evidently he was related to the Judds in some way. They had sat up all evening, playing music and talking, and when it was getting on toward dawn they started hearing drums.

Of course, most of the people here knew what the drums meant. He didn't and he asked questions, but all he got was evasive answers. "Well, it's just people practicing in the back of the valley." That sort of thing. He had been in the back of the valley. He knew nobody lived there.

So he wanted to go and see for himself. People told him to stay put, but he went rambling off by himself and he didn't come back. At daylight they went looking for him. They found him in the middle of the trail with his mouth wide open and his eyes wide open, and his fingers bent back, apparently dead of a heart attack.

Other people tell me that the trail crosses Kamehameha Highway and that there are a lot of car accidents in that area. A lot of them just happen to occur on the night of Kāne. Some people attribute it to a bad curve, but I think there's something else going on.

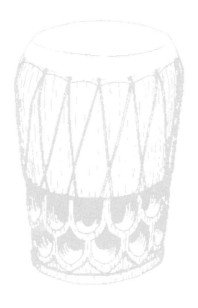

Anonymous lives on Oʻahu. Credit, he says, should go to the *kanaka maoli* who told him this story. "Night Marchers of Kualoa" originally appeared as an oral history in *Nā Moʻolelo ʻŌkala: Eerie Stories from Hawaiʻi,* a senior honors thesis by Jean Kent Campbell.

Sky, Sea, Earth

The Three Storms of Hina

Thoughts for a Dead Japanese Fisherman

The Woman Who Talks to Rocks

For one whole year dancers of Hālau Mohala 'Ilima practiced "The Three Storms of Hina" in preparation for the Merrie Monarch Hula Festival. They learned every nuance of the *hula kahiko* and chant, perhaps too well. As they danced in competition on a rainy night in Hilo, the sky broke with lightning and thunder and the lights went out. Shaken, the hula dancers gave up their chance to win rather than risk the wrath of . . .

The Three Storms of Hina

Are you superstitious? Do you believe some things just cannot be explained? Do you believe in the gods and goddesses that are a part of Hawai'i's folklore?

I never considered myself to be a superstitious person. If I searched hard enough, certainly I would find an explanation for everything. I grew up listening to the legends my *kupuna* told. The gods and goddesses in these stories belonged to a time that was behind me and these legends were a record of all thing's past. Things from my ancestors' past would never belong to the present, so I gave little thought to any of it—not until one night in April 1986.

I was one of 24 dancers of Hālau Mohala 'Ilima and we were in Hilo for the Merrie Monarch Hula Festival. We were a close-knit group, and after nine months of training together, we were ready to share our hula with the crowd gathered at the Edith Kanaka'ole Stadium. Our *kumu*, Māpuana de Silva, and her husband, Kīhei, had prepared us well, and we were excited to be participating in the "Olympics" of hula.

The *hula kahiko* competition number, which eighteen *wahine* groups were going to present, was "Pu'inokolu'a Hina" (The Three Storms of Hina). The chant speaks of Hina, the goddess who guards the island of Moloka'i.

Hina keeps the sacred wind gourd, "Wawahonua," and

when the people mistreat the land, she opens the gourd slightly to release its first storm. "Trees are uprooted and thrown over . . . shrubbery is twirled, sweeping down and out to sea." Hina waits for the people to improve, but they don't. Hina opens the gourd cover halfway to release the second, stronger storm, "causing skies to darken . . . lightning flashes, thunder cracks . . . wild gushes of wind causing ocean floods." There is little change in the hearts of the people, so Hina opens the gourd cover all the way and "the worse storm is released; crushed are the chief, crushed is the land." (Of the three winds associated with the storms—'Ilinahu, Uluhewa and Luluku—only the last one, Luluku, is a destroyer of man. This final destruction is how Hina protects her beloved land of Moloka'i).[1]

The weather in Hilo during the Festival of 1986 was unlike the weather of previous years. Yes, Hilo has a lot of rain, but this time it was different. As I recall, during the Miss Aloha Hula competition on Thursday night, there was a soft breeze blowing through the stadium and the rain was nothing but a light mist. Nothing seemed unusual. The Hilo rains continued all day Friday, and by Friday night the rain was coming down a little harder, the wind was picking up, and things were looking a little ominous.

As we dressed and prepared for our performance, we could hear the other *hālau* take their turn on stage. With every performance, the weather seemed to worsen. I wondered if there was a connection between what was happening on stage and the weather conditions. Were the dancers merely telling a story or were they becoming the storm? The chanting and dancing continued, and the storm intensified. The pelting rain was now accompanied by strong

---

[1] Description taken from Kīhei de Silva, "Hula Kahiko—Pu'inokolu'a Hina," *Merrie Monarch Fact Sheet.*

gusty winds, spectacular shows of bright lightning, and deafening sounds of thunder. I began to feel uncomfortable.

I sat alone and thought about this chant and remembered the difficulty I had in mastering the dance, difficulty I had never experienced with any of the other chants I learned over the years. I didn't enjoy this chant or this dance because I was having such a hard time. During our performance we would be taking the role of storytellers and focusing on the love Hina has for the land. We would not, in our dance, become those three storms. The dance we learned was to be done with calmness, but I never felt calm.

My thoughts were interrupted when the lights went out just before the intermission. We were dressed and ready to perform, but there would now be an indefinite delay. I remember a strange silence at first and then the emcees were doing their best to distract the crowd of 5,000. My hula sisters and I formed a circle under the bleachers with Māpu, Kīhei and Aunty Nana Kalama as the audience began to sing a song I don't remember. We held hands and talked about how we were feeling at that moment. After Māpu, Kīhei and Aunty Nana left the circle to have a discussion of their own, my hula sisters and I decided that we did not want to dance. I remember being the one to tell Māpu that we were uncomfortable about performing and I remember the look of complete understanding and concern in her eyes. Māpu put our well-being above all else and was sensitive to our feelings. About an hour later the lights went on and the Festival resumed. When Hālau Mohala 'Ilima was introduced, Māpu went onto the stage and told the captive audience that we would not be performing that night because it would be inappropriate for us. She returned to our group and we could feel the strength of our conviction and the love all of us had for each other. It seemed as if the intensity of the chant was disrupted. For the first time that night, many of us finally felt peace.

After a brief moment, the next *hālau* was introduced and called to the stage. The dancers of Hālau Mohala ʻIlima were putting their costumes away. There was a light breeze blowing through the stadium and the rain was nothing but a soft mist. The storm had suddenly ended. The elements were calm.

Lei-Ann Stender Durant, a former Merrie Monarch dancer with Hālau Mohala ʻIlima, didn't dance that year at the festival. She is a member of the first *ʻūniki* class of the *hālau* and a graduated *kumu*. A mother of two, she is not active in hula right now.

Pele Visits Mauna Loa

When Puʻu ʻŌʻō first erupted, I think it was 1983, there was a big eruption and there was a group of Leilehua High students filming. On their video camera they are all talking while they're filming and just mumbling, you know, "the volcano is doing this and that." All of a sudden you can hear, "Oh, shit, look at that." What they were watching was this fireball, this ball of light crossing the sky like a meteor went over. It lit up the sky like you wouldn't believe. It looked like it went over the top of Mauna Loa. Within seconds the top of Mauna Loa erupted. Of course to a lot of people that was Madame Pele leaving one site to go start another one.

Contributed by Anonymous; originally appeared as an oral history in *Nā Moʻolelo ʻŌkala: Eerie Stories from Hawaiʻi,* a senior honors thesis by Jean Kent Campbell.

Her parents divorced when she was small. She grew up never really knowing her father. He was distant, remote. They were *tsuki* to *suppon*. Moon and turtle. Both round, little else in common. She wanted a different father. He wanted a different daughter. Years later, after her father died doing what he loved best— fishing—an island woman discovers that "the spirits of the dead will all come back," as she is surrounded by the memory of her father and the common threads of their lives in . . .

Thoughts for a Dead Japanese Fisherman

It is said in ancient Japanese folklore that one who drowns returns to life as a sea animal. As I run along the beach, I look for my father. But today the ocean is like flat unfolded sheets of origami. I know he is out there. Perhaps he is a turtle, an *'ahi*, a shark, a manta ray, a mackerel or a tuna. He is out there.

It has been 18 years since his last breath. *Iki o hikitoru.*

I still remember the telephone call from my older sister, March 27, 1977. I was visiting old college roommates in Menlo Park, California. Asad, my Pakistani friend, was attempting to teach me country-western dancing. We were in the middle of the living room, having moved all of the mismatched furniture off to the side. Asad was tall, slender and dark brown like a *sakura no ki*. Cherry tree, I thought to myself.

He showed me the pattern once more. Four steps forward. Count the beats. Arms crossed over me like branches. Get ready for a twirl. But my feet were filled with thoughts of their own.

Just as on that day, my feet move on their own today. But they are careful always to dance out of the reach of the sea.

The music hung in the air like colored Japanese paper lanterns strung along wires on August nights. Laughter clustered like waiting bon dancers in their silk kimonos, *yukata* and happi coats around the red, white and gold *yagura*, or musician's tower. It was at that moment the telephone rang. Asad dropped my arm to answer the phone. The cherry blossoms or *sakura-no hana* floated downward, becoming a lighted candle on the River of the Dead.

He turned to me, holding the telephone out.

"I think it is for you. I can't understand her too well."

Even without putting my ear to the telephone, I could hear the woman sobbing, deep and hoarse. Like pain coming from the belly of the earth that has just been split. *Hara o waru.*

"You have to come home."

In that moment I knew it was either my mother or my father. Please, let it be my father that has died, I prayed.

And so it was. *Oboreta.* Drowned. He died doing what he loved best—fishing.

I stop to catch my breath. I look out over the immense ocean. But there is no movement, no sign. The origami sea lies untouched. It is like every Sunday morning for the past eighteen years. I continue running.

There is no wind down there. No wind to fly carps. Without wind there is no sound and nothing ages, just like the memories that the living have of the dead.

The waves wash higher, clutching more sand. The sands are pulled down. Even the waves change from day to day. But not Papa. He is forever forty-nine. No jellyfish-white strands among his black hair.

Yesterday, a two-year-old girl drowned at Magic Island. Day after day, her mother and father will only see the child that was. Always with the same smile, always accompanied by the same favorite cuddly animal, always dressed in the same clothes. Always two.

Two weeks ago, a German tourist stood with his back to

the Blow Hole. The wave pulled him into the sea as he stood there smiling. His family watching in horror, waiting for the sea to spit his body back out. They finally found him late that afternoon, his body washed up in a nearby cave. A family who came to vacation and returned home to mourn.

The young surfer was never found. His family's dreams broken like the remains of his board, which washed up on shore the next morning.

The old Chinese man picking *'opihi.* He never had a chance. He never knew how to swim.

But the *tamashii,* or spirits of the dead, will all come back. *Pāpio, onaga, aku,* eel, *tai* or red snapper, sea cucumber—

Like my father.

The ocean waves cough up a *liliko'i* and roll it up on the sand. White and smooth it reminds me of a cue ball. My own two sons will never know their Japanese grandfather who tried vainly to teach his hardheaded daughter to play billiards with a soft touch.

"Don't whack the balls," he'd grimace as I sent the white cue ball spinning forward with all my sixteen-year-old might. Some of the solid and striped balls would jump off the pool table. I wanted that. I thought it showed *chikara,* or strength. He shook his head. "You get more if you are gentle."

I never knew what that meant. I was *ishi atama.* Rock head. I didn't listen to him when he gave me that advice. Not once did I ever take his advice.

Tsuki to suppon. Moon and turtle. Although both round, we shared nothing else in common.

I wanted a different father. He wanted a different daughter. Peach blossom, not *kuchi no heranai hito.* Smart aleck.

Some days not even our curves matched. We were like the old samurai saying: *Sori ga awanai.* In the old days, samurai wore their swords at their side. If the curved shape of the sheath, or *sori*, did not match (*awanai*) the curve of the sword, it could not be used. And we could not see eye to eye, especially not about my future.

I wanted to be somebody and do something. I wanted to leave the Islands, especially Wahiawā, and live on the mainland. I didn't want to be "the frog in the well who knows nothing of the great ocean beyond." *I no naka no kawazu taikai o shirazu.* So I didn't listen to him when he said I didn't need to attend law school in Washington, D.C.

"You know enough big words." It was that same shake of his head that I had seen when I was sixteen. He knew I would not listen.

That's the only thing he ever said about me going to law school. Yes, I learned lots of big words that first year in law school. Fancy Latin words—*caveat emptor, res ipsa loquitur, nunc pro tunc.* None of them meant anything, though, when we arranged the funeral. Coffin, cremation, burial. Everyone knows the meaning of those words.

He was the salt of the ocean. A man whose high school yearbook slogan read "not to be known." His needs were simple. The tide calendar nailed above his bed was his only appointment book.

Mizu no awa. As I watch the foam bubbles float on the water, I think maybe now we have more in common.

Maybe we both feel regret. Each of us drinking our own tears for lives that did not work out as planned. *Namida o nomu.* Maybe he is still a fisherman—only now he fishes for souls.

Every May we raise the *koi-nobori*. Loaded with red, blue and black flying carp leaping in the wind, the bamboo pole is a beacon. So my father will know I have two boys. And they would be very good fishermen, if I ever would let them get close to the sea.

Leslie Ann Hayashi, a graduate of Leilehua High School, studied broadcast journalism at Stanford University but "somehow ended up in law school." She is now a district court judge in Honolulu. "Thoughts for a Dead Japanese Fisherman," a tribute to her father, was the 1995 Grand Prize Winner in the *Honolulu Magazine*/Borders Books & Music Fiction Contest.

While Hawai'i is part of the United States, it continues to be part of Polynesia, connected by a much older set of loyalties to the island clusters and people farther south—the Marquesas, Sāmoa, Tonga, Tahiti, the Maori of Aotearoa (sometimes called New Zealand) and Rapa Nui, or Easter Island. Polynesians have known all along that these places are alive and need to be listened to. In Hawai'i, author James D. Houston writes, many people believe it is possible to communicate with rocks. I often talk to rocks in Hawai'i and elsewhere in Polynesia, usually while hiking, but unlike the rock of Nānākuli in this unnerving story, not one has ever talked back.

The Woman Who Talks to Rocks

On my way to the Big Island, I stop off in Honolulu to have breakfast with a woman who talks to rocks. She is an 80-year-old Hawaiian woman with thick white hair and a healer's eyes. Over papaya and Kona coffee, she describes a conversation with a very large and influential rock near the town of Nānākuli on the leeward side of O'ahu where the county was clearing land for a new dump site.

An odd sequence of events had begun to trouble the construction crew. Tools had unaccountably disappeared, vehicles were breaking down. A shallow-rooted *kiawe* tree had flipped over, doing a kind of somersault. A worker was thrown when a flat stone suddenly up-ended itself.

In Hawai'i, when things like this start to happen, you don't take chances. You seek expert advice, usually from an elder who is in tune with the visible and invisible life of the region. So this woman was called in to look around and see what she could see and feel what she could feel.

"I stood there awhile and prayed," she tells me, "and when I opened my eyes, I noticed this rock I had not seen at first. It was a large rock, as large as this table"—spreading her hands wide. "I said to that rock, 'Who are you?' and the rock replied that it held the *'aumakua* of that place, the guardian spirit. So I told the workmen that such a rock should not be lying on its side. It should be standing upright and they did that, they set it up straight. And I went away, thinking that the problem at the dump site had been solved."

This woman's voice, as soft and as smooth as a flower petal, has a soothing mesmerizing quality. As she pauses halfway through her story to signal for more coffee, I am hearing another voice, that of a fellow in my neighborhood at home who asks me a question each time I get ready to leave for these islands. With a few variations it is always the same question:

"What do you really do over there?" he wants to know, his voice tinged with suspicious curiosity. I never know quite how to reply. He imagines me stretched out on the sand at water's edge sipping mai tais and baking in the sun for days on end. Thirty-five years ago that image would not have been too far from the truth. On my first trip to these islands, the beaches and the surf were powerful magnets. Jeanne and I were married on the beach, with Diamond Head in the distance, and with Hawaiian music, just as the sun was going down. So there are sentimental reasons. Nowadays there are also professional reasons. The last time I was accosted by this neighbor of mine, I told him, "If you really want to know, it's a business trip. I have a magazine assignment."

I knew he didn't believe me. That is, he didn't want to believe this was the real reason for the trip. And of course he was right. But I didn't know how to tell him this without mentioning the rocks, which would have meant watching his eyes narrow with much more than suspicion. I would have had to watch his face say silently that I was losing my grip. In his world, which is the one most of us inhabit on the mainland—a world ruled by software and satellites and credit cards—rocks have no powers. They certainly cannot talk. How then could I explain to him that

I actually enjoy being in a place where rocks still have a life of their own? How could I tell him that if I had to name the many things calling me back year after year—the romance, the light, the color, the music, the dance—if I named them all, rocks would be right on the top of the list?

Out near Nānākuli strange things kept happening. Before long the foreman at the construction site summoned her again. She knew she had to confront that *'aumakua* rock, so she went right to it and said, "What do you want?"

"I want to be higher," the rock replied.

"Why do you want to be up higher?"

"I should not be here. This place is defiled."

The rock, she told them, would have to be moved. The next morning the foreman arrived at her house at 4 a.m. "We had to get there and do all the moving before sunup," she explains, "while the energy of the day was on the rise."

When they reached the site a truck was there, and around it stood ten men from the crew who had also set their alarms for 4 a.m. They were waiting to be told where to relocate that rock.

"Up higher," she said, pointing to a ridge. "Up there."

They hoisted it onto the truck bed and clambered aboard. The truck began to climb, following a little-used road that leads to a Hawaiian Electric Co. relay station. They reached the ridge in time to unload the rock before the sun cleared the mountain range behind them. They placed it in a setting of smaller stones, facing west, with a view of the valley below and Oʻahu's leeward shoreline. After the woman blessed the new site and left an offering of ti leaves at the base of the rock, they all drove down the relay station access road and that was the end of the crew's trouble as well as the end of her story.

"After that, they didn't have to call 'em back."

On the mainland this will sound far-fetched, but in the vol-canically formed and lava-conscious islands of Hawai'i you hear such stories all the time. This story happened to be reported on page one of the *Honolulu Advertiser*. . . . Why was it on page one? Because Hawai'i is a place where quite a few people believe it is possible to communicate with rocks. You also find people who claim to communi-cate with trees, with the wind and with the mountains, as well as the creatures who inhabit the mountains and swim in the sea. There is a long tradition of doing this, and in my view these are examples of a very important kind of dia-logue—the respectful dialogue between human beings and all the other features of our natural surroundings.

In the world most of us inhabit now it is easy to lose touch with this dialogue. But when there are stories to remind you that the rock has life, it can help you to remember that the mountain has a life and the island has a life. . . .

James D. Houston, novelist, editor, and film writer, is co-author with Ben Finney of *Surfing: A History of the Ancient Hawaiian Sport*. With his wife, Jeanne Wakatsuki Houston, he wrote *Farewell to Manzanar*, the story of her family's experiences during and after the World War II internment of Japanese Americans. A former Wallace Stegner Writing Fellow at Stanford University, Houston is the author of fifteen works of fiction and nonfiction including *California: Searching for the Golden State*. His articles on Hawai'i have appeared in the *New York Times, San Francisco Chronicle, Honolulu,* and *Mānoa*. "The Women Who Talks to Rocks" will appear in his new book, *The Steaming World Sojourns in the Ring of Fire*, due in April 1997 from Mercury House, San Francisco. He lives in Santa Cruz, California.